BEYOND TROCHENBROD

BEYOND TROCHENBROD

The Betty Gold Story

✳ ✳ ✳

Betty Gold

with Mark Hodermarsky

✳ ✳ ✳

THE KENT STATE UNIVERSITY PRESS   KENT, OHIO

© 2014 by The Kent State University Press, Kent, Ohio 44242
ALL RIGHTS RESERVED
Library of Congress Catalog Card Number 2013042807
ISBN 978-1-60635-199-4
Manufactured in the United States of America

LIBRARY OF CONGRESS CATALOGING-IN-PUBLICATION DATA
Gold, Betty, 1930– author.
Beyond Trochenbrod : the Betty Gold story /
Betty Gold with Mark Hodermarsky.
Includes bibliographical references and index.
ISBN 978-1-60635-199-4 (pbk.) ∞
1. Gold, Betty, 1930– 2. Jews—Ukraine—Sofiivka (Volyns'ka oblast')—
Biography. 3. Holocaust, Jewish (1939–1945)—Ukraine—Sofiivka
(Volyns'ka oblast')—Personal narratives. 4. Holocaust survivors—
Ohio—Cleveland—Biography. 5. Sofiivka (Volyns'ka oblast', Ukraine)—
Biography. I. Hodermarsky, Mark, author. II. Title.
DS135.U43G6374 2014
940.53'18092—dc23
[B]
2013042807

18 17 16 15 14   5 4 3 2 1

For the victims of

the Trochenbrod Massacre

and Nancy Wilhelm

✳ ✳ ✳

"The only way to overcome sadness is to consume it."

—Jonathan Safran Foer

(*Everything Is Illuminated*)

CONTENTS

PREFACE

Mark Hodermarsky

Near Nobel Peace Prize recipient, author, and Holocaust survivor, Elie Wiesel, sat a petite woman whose dark eyes and pensive expression devoured the guest speaker's every word. Wiesel, addressing the Saint Ignatius High School student body, was discussing his book *Night*, a terrifying memoir of his confinement with his father at the Auschwitz and Buchenwald concentration camps in 1944 and 1945. At the time, I knew only her name, Betty Gold, and that she was a local Holocaust survivor. Within a few months, however, Betty and I would be immersed in writing her unforgettable story.

Nancy Wilhelm, a history teacher at Saint Ignatius in Cleveland, had invited Betty to speak to her classes before Wiesel's 2007 visit. Having taken students on field trips to the Maltz Museum of Jewish Heritage in Beachwood, a suburb of Cleveland, where Betty then and now serves as a docent, Nancy witnessed Betty's riveting narrative about the tragic events at her home, Trochenbrod, once a prosperous Polish town whose population was 99 percent Jewish. Nancy felt compelled to introduce her to the Saint Ignatius community. Betty would return to the campus regularly, not only to talk to Nancy's classes but to others and eventually to mine. It was Nancy who asked me to consider helping Betty put her story into words, the story she had been sharing with so many for so long.

Before committing to the project, I asked Betty to visit one of my English classes, and that's all it took. In my thirty-eight years of teaching, I have never seen a class so transfixed by a guest speaker as on that memorable day. The young men were touched by Betty's dramatic and poignant testimony to the point of tears. I decided, right then and there, that I must help Betty write her story.

And it is Betty's story, her memory of what took place, that I've attempted to recount from our many interviews over several years. The memoir's tone is conversational rather than scholarly. My goal has been to preserve Betty's distinctive voice, to replicate in print what has enlightened and inspired those who have heard her speak.

It has taken Betty and many Holocaust survivors quite a few years to tell their stories, even to family members. Not until Steven Spielberg founded the Survivors of the Shoah Visual History Foundation was Betty willing to discuss her past. Between 1994 and 1999, Spielberg's foundation conducted thousands of video interviews with Holocaust survivors like Betty Gold. Betty began to describe in depth the Trochenbrod massacre, her harrowing escape from the Nazis, and the subsequent brutal physical and psychological hardships that she and her family endured while hiding in the forest. Increasingly driven to disclose the atrocities that were committed against her beloved townspeople, Betty, in 2005, accepted the chance to volunteer as a docent at the Maltz Museum. The popularity of Betty's absorbing talks eventually led to speaking engagements at high schools, colleges, and organizations.

Recently, Avrom Bendavid-Val authored a book on Trochenbrod, *The Heavens Are Empty;* Jeremy Goldsheider produced a film documentary on Trochenbrod, *Lost Town;* and *Everything Is Illuminated* by Jonathan Safran Foer became a critically acclaimed fictional account of Trochenbrod that was also made into a popular movie. All three men have relied on Betty Gold for their projects, and she has been extraordinarily pleased by the results. As the only living survivor of the Trochenbrod tragedy, her vocation has been to ensure that the world does not forget the evil that was inflicted upon her Polish town, now a barren stretch of land in Ukraine that she has visited on three occasions. As Betty has expressed on countless occasions, "We must educate, learn, and never forget the atrocities of the Holocaust. It is the only way to prevent it from happening again." This has been her mission statement.

Among many unforgettable features of Betty's narrative is the courage she demonstrated as a child, including her willingness to scavenge alone for food at night at enormous risk to herself and her family. That a twelve-year-old girl was given such immense responsibility for the group's survival is remarkable. Added to these gripping childhood experiences are her details regarding the challenges that awaited her upon her arrival to America in 1946, especially the prejudices she faced as a Jewish immigrant and as a woman. Later, she shares the heartrending events of a broken marriage, surviving cancer, and losing two adult sons, one by suicide.

Though Betty might be expected to feel bitterness and anger, she has displayed instead perseverance, wisdom, and compassion. She has gone beyond her experiences in Trochenbrod to transform hearts and minds. Betty Gold has embraced life, both the good and bad it offers all of us.

INTRODUCTION

Mark Hodermarsky

Nothing remains of Trochenbrod. A prosperous Polish town of five thousand exists only in memory. The shopkeepers, craftspeople, teachers, factory workers, and farmers are all silent. Synagogues, Hebrew school, leather factories, and retail shops have been replaced by a tractor trail, barren fields, and scattered stones. In fact, the former town no longer belongs to eastern Poland; it is now part of northwestern Ukraine, near Lutsk.

Trochenbrod, the Yiddish name for a Russian town called Sofiyovka in Ukrainian and Zofiowka in Polish, was founded in 1835 as a Jewish settlement. Legend has it that it was named after the first two Jews to live in the town: Trochaen and Brod. The Polish names derive from Sofia, a Russian princess who donated land for the settlement. To avoid oppressive anti-Jewish laws in Tsarist Russia, including having sons serve in the Russian army until the age of forty-five, Jews poured into Trochenbrod, making it the only all-Jewish town to exist outside biblical Israel. Eventually, Jews would make up 99 percent of the population.

Following the First World War, the town fell from Russian hands into Polish control, and Trochenbrod thrived. Eli Potash, Betty Gold's father, became a successful proprietor of a leatherworking shop, supplying the townspeople and peasants with shoes, boots, and saddles. Eli and Riva Potash, along with their three children, lived comfortably in a six-room house. Except for a few instances of anti-Semitism, Betty Potash Gold, through age nine, enjoyed a happy childhood, surrounded by a loving and large extended family. The serenity, however, was about to end—swiftly and horrifically.

At the outbreak of the Second World War in 1939, Germany and the Soviet Union conquered Poland, placing Trochenbrod under Soviet rule. In July 1941, Germany betrayed its ally and invaded the Soviet Union. Betty Gold remembers: "My parents and other adults told me that during the First World War, we Trochenbroders were treated relatively well by the occupying Austrian-Hungarian, German-speaking army. As a result, we did not anticipate any rough treatment from the current German forces." Many ethnic Ukrainians, too, initially welcomed the Germans. But there were signs that the Nazi occupation of Trochenbrod would soon alter any favorable impressions.

Gold had heard stories from refugees of western Poland that Jews were being killed by Nazis in some places, but the desire and will to kill peasants seemed incomprehensible to an eleven-year-old: "What could be gained? Why bother to inflict such acts of violence on such a small, insignificant town? Trochenbrod is not Warsaw." In the summer of 1942, however, it became clear that the Nazis indeed had devised treacherous plans when one day they ordered all of Trochenbrod's Jews to leave their homes and walk to the center of town. From here they were transferred two miles by trucks to the edge of the forest.

On August 11, one day after her twelfth birthday, while hiding with fifteen others in a secret partition that her father had built onto the shed, Gold escaped a nightmarish fate. After the Nazis and their auxiliary police had completed digging trenches to be used as a mass grave, 4,500 Jews—including Gold's grandmother, aunts, uncles, and cousins—were lined up and machine-gunned by a Nazi death squad known as Einsatzgruppe C. Eventually, Gold's family escaped to the surrounding woods, where they miraculously survived until a group of Soviet partisans found them in the fall of 1943 and, five months later, brought them to a collective farm.

In the following pages, Betty Gold describes how she and her family managed to endure the challenges of hunger, thirst, pain, fear, and complete despair. Man's inhumanity is apparent in Gold's narrative but so is man's capacity to prevail in spite of unimaginable odds.

CHAPTER ONE

TROCHENBROD

✳ As often happened in villages throughout Poland in 1921, my mother, Riva Tepper, was quite young, only seventeen, when she married my father, Eli Potash, who was himself just nineteen. Riva and Eli became parents soon after their marriage. In 1923, a son was born, Shiman, followed by Bernard in 1928, and then me in 1930. Between the two boys, my parents suffered the loss of a stillborn, another boy.

Both of my parents were born in Trochenbrod, met in Trochenbrod, raised a family in Trochenbrod, and, if fate had not stepped in, would have most likely died and been buried in the town. With few exceptions, that was the cycle of most villagers' lives.

The townspeople had a comparatively pleasant life. Contributing to a natural sense of stability and comfort was the fact that 99 percent of the five thousand residents of Trochenbrod were Jewish. A strong work ethic and fertile soil, combined with the shared customs and Jewish values, helped to create a thriving community. Dairy farms, leather factories, a glass factory, retail shops, school buildings, and synagogues dotted the landscape, employing farmers, tradesmen, clerks, teachers, and rabbis. Trochenbrod's industrious and prosperous farmers and merchants were of great importance to the surrounding Polish and Ukrainian villages.

My father, the hardest-working man I've ever known, typified this entrepreneurial spirit. At nineteen, he was already making a living as a leatherworker, supporting both his family and his parents. As a deaf mute, Eli's father, Nusin, understandably had difficulty being an effective provider. My father also tirelessly spoiled my mother.

With her raven hair, dark brown eyes, and porcelain complexion, my beautiful mother was put on a pedestal by her husband. Eli treated Riva like a Polish princess. He made certain that his wife dressed well, that she did a minimal amount of housework and cooking, and that she occasionally be allowed to visit a spa in Czechoslovakia. Perhaps it was my mother's ill health that led Father to pamper her as she suffered from stomach problems throughout her life, some of which I may have inherited.

I'm sure that she respected my father, but I don't think my mother loved my father as much as he loved her. Sometimes I felt that my mother took advantage of him. She wasn't overly demanding, and I don't recall her ever complaining to him, but he tried so hard to please her that I couldn't help but feel some resentment toward her. It would have been nice had she said no sometimes to him, "No, I don't want this; no, I don't need this."

I didn't get along as well with my mother as I did with my father. I suppose I was stubborn and didn't like her constantly telling me what to do. She seemed to be critical of me—and only rarely approved of my actions. Likewise, I resented her getting sick because my father had to take care of her. Maybe I was jealous of her. I don't know.

Yet my mother, to her credit, always tried to improve herself. Even though she had not attended school, she learned to read Yiddish. Trochenbrod's library, where my mother regularly sent me for books, was practically next door. Unlike many Trochenbrod women, she loved to read and was knowledgeable on a wide range of topics. She also was a contributing member of the community and did a lot of organizational work for a number of activities. Mother liked to be involved and, I think, relished the attention that came with her participation. I must admit that I inherited this trait from her. My mother was a very shrewd and smart lady. I admired her strength, ambition, and self-confidence. She wanted to be more than a Trochenbrod

This is a photograph of me at age three in 1933.

lady. She wanted to be noticed. Maybe she dreamed of becoming an esteemed lady from a big city rather than an unknown woman from a sleepy, small town.

With a six-room home and more than an acre of land, my family lived well compared to most others in the village. Because she didn't have to work as hard as did other Trochenbrod women, Mother was envied by most ladies. True, most women, except for a teacher or dressmaker, stayed home as housekeepers. But my mother didn't labor as exhaustively as did her peers, relying instead on her mother-in-law, Nechama, to assist with the cooking and a hired housekeeper to occasionally clean and do laundry. Even though I understood why they perceived my mother as spoiled, I became upset at their attitude toward her.

My mother clearly displayed her status as a woman of prestige by the girth of her waistline. She was obviously well fed, reflecting a household supported by a financially successful husband. In those days, society equated a plump wife with a prosperous home. How things have changed today, when the opposite perception is held—certainly in America.

Dad was a man of principle. Eli never told anybody how to live his or her life, and he didn't want to be told how to live his life. "Leave me alone and I'll leave you alone" seemed to be his motto. A private man, he neither gossiped nor wished to interfere in anyone's personal life. He enjoyed the company of others, but he wasn't a card player or gambler or drinker. My mother, on the other hand, enjoyed playing cards with both men and women. Unlike Father, she loved to socialize. He did a lot of shopping for groceries. His main outlet was the synagogue, where he joined the brotherhood of the faithful. Father was quite involved with the men's association, which focused primarily on the religious education of children.

Dad was a very religious man who honored every Sabbath and Jewish holiday. Seemingly everyone in Trochenbrod was religious, although only a few men (if any) were strongly orthodox. Except for the rabbis, most men did not wear beards. Nor was it essential that girls or children attend synagogue. My father prayed devoutly for thirty minutes each morning and night and attended synagogue each Saturday and holiday. My mother, on the other hand, did not show similar devotion to her faith. She was more contemporary and less traditional in many ways than my father.

Skillfully fashioning leather into shoes, boots, belts, coin purses, reins, and saddles took up most of my father's time. The shop, which he built himself, proved to be a successful enterprise as he dedicated himself relentlessly toward supporting his family. A handy carpenter as well as leatherworker, Father also built a house for his parents at the back of his store after building our own house. Keeping his wife and family well fed and clothed was his chief vocation. Dad was a craftsman, preferring to employ his hands rather than his intellect. Mom read while Dad labored.

As I've stated, I was closer to my father than I was to my mother. While my mother slept, I would get up in the morning and eat breakfast—usually hot cereal—with Dad. Before we went to school and to work, roughly a mile from home, my father and I would make sandwiches for our lunches consisting of cheese or chicken fat with kosher salt and bread, along with a fruit or vegetable. Then, holding hands, we began our walk. After we kissed each other good-bye in front of his leatherworking shop, I went on to school.

This daily ritual strengthened our inseparable bond. I treasured these mornings as much as I've treasured anything in life—Dad and I simply sharing breakfast and a walk, talking and laughing, and enjoying each other's company.

While my father favored me, my mother favored my younger brother, Bernard. She was extremely close to him. And so was Adel, her mother. Bernie practically lived with his grandmother, who lived across the street from us. I looked up to my older brother, Shiman, who was seven years older than me. Unlike Shiman, who grew to six feet, Bernard never fully grew because of the Holocaust and remained at five foot seven. My father stood at five foot eleven while my mother was taller than me at five foot four. I never grew beyond five feet.

Shiman was a gentle young man with a sweet disposition. He took after my father, and I resembled my mother. (If you saw my mother in one town and then me the next day in another town, you would say, "I think I saw your mother yesterday. Do you have a mother there?" People would recognize me from miles away. I looked exactly like her.) Despite our age difference, Shiman spent much time with me. I looked up to him immensely. To this day, I can't fathom why my dear father treated Shiman the way he did.

My father was a responsible and decent man. I idolized him and modeled my life after his in many ways: not buying unless you have the money, saving a penny to a penny, and working hard. "You can accomplish anything you wish through hard work." That was the code he lived by.

The only thing I can't figure out was his treatment of my older brother. I watched as Dad physically abused Shiman. I would cry, but my tears did not stop the beatings. I would run to Shiman, who would hide in terror, in an effort to comfort him after these attacks. I don't know why my father would beat up such a sensitive, kind boy. I never learned what Shiman did

Pictured here are Grandmother Adel and my parents, Eli and Riva Potash, in the early 1920s.

to deserve such punishment. Shiman never got into trouble. He was respectful of his parents and others. I know that during that era children were often disciplined in this way, but it never made any sense.

Why Shiman? Father never laid a hand on me or Bernard. I was emotionally torn because of my love for my father and brother. I adored my dad, but I never fully understood nor forgave him for hitting Shiman. Of all the events of my childhood leading up to our escape from the Nazis, this was my most emotionally disturbing experience.

Bernie was a feisty little guy. He was a lot fun and quite a character. He thoroughly enjoyed life as a happy-go-lucky kid. Unlike Shiman, Bernie would occasionally play some tricks and break some rules. Yom Kippur is the holiest day in the Jewish religion. You're not supposed to do anything. You fast and you pray all day. I remember one time I was outside, and he broke

Mother, Father, and Bernie are seen here in Nowostan, Poland, a vacation resort, in 1932.

a stick—a stick—what's the big deal? Anyway, I squealed on him because he had violated a sacred tenet. At that time, I was very orthodox and more like my father. I told on Bernie, who simply laughed at me for taking something so insignificant so seriously. Of course, he wasn't punished. And he lived his adult life the same way. He was just a good-natured, joyful man with a wonderful sense of humor. Everyone, including Father, got along well with Bernie.

Trochenbrod, overwhelmingly Jewish since its founding in 1835 as a Jewish settlement, had only one Christian family— Janina Lubinski, the town's postmistress, and Ryszard, her son, who was my age. Under Polish law, the postmaster could not be Jewish. They lived next door to my father's shop. Ryszard and I were like brother and sister, and we played together. He even thought he was Jewish because everyone spoke Jewish, and he lived in a town of all Jews. During Christmas time Ryszard invited his Jewish friends to his home to see the Lubinskis' Christmas tree. We loved touching and smelling that tree.

Anti-Semitism crept into our lives when Christians from the surrounding villages attended Sunday church service. Most of the parishioners had to pass through our town and that was one day when we all remained inside. Children were kept off the streets until the churchgoers left our village and returned to their homes. Some of the male parishioners stopped at the liquor store, which was owned by a Gentile, on their way back from service and got drunk. Even if they weren't drunk, they looked for opportunities to taunt and beat up Jewish children and adults. I remember my parents warning me, "You might get hit. You might get beaten up. Stay in the house." In some of the village shops, I recall hearing a Christian customer using the expression "dirty Jew." But these occasions were infrequent.

We celebrated all the Jewish holidays. Those were blissful times from which I cherish wonderful memories. On the holidays we would gather at temple, although, to be honest, children didn't come to pray but to socialize. On Sabbath my father would go to temple, and, when he returned, we all would share a meal together. Following a meat-and-potatoes dinner, we would rest for a while and then go to the park, where other people were meeting and relaxing and having fun. I miss those rituals terribly. And as hard as I have tried to keep up these traditions here, it's not the same. When I started my own family many years later, I tried to recreate these and other Jewish customs from my youth.

Trochenbrod was a community—one big family. Everybody in town was either related or a neighbor. You knew everybody. I remember Friday nights when Sabbath started and all of the Trochenbrod women began lighting candles. Prayers followed and then we would eat and sing religious songs. And with the windows opened in the summer, you could hear everyone in town singing the same songs—one big family at one great meal.

The weather in eastern Poland was temperate, much like the climate in the Midwestern United States and the weather in Cleveland. We enjoyed warm summers and cold winters. Nearby were woods, pasturelands, lakes, marshes, and hills.

Our small village—*shtetl*—was roughly seventeen thousand acres. The town had only one main unpaved road, but the people made the most of the village's small dimensions. Most Trochenbroders owned enough land behind their homes in which to plant some crops. We would plant cucumbers, tomatoes, beans, radishes, and onions. The entire family would be involved in the planting and harvesting of the vegetables.

Bernie and I used to love to plant flowers in front of our home, and I remember one summer we planted some little blue flowers that smelled beautiful. We even shaped these flowers to form the initials of our names. We opened our windows at night so that we could breathe in their intoxicating scents. I'll always remember that garden and all the lovely landscapes of my town.

Trochenbrod could not expand because of the woods that surrounded it. As children we often wandered into Radziwill Forest, named after a renowned Polish prince who owned the forest. We used to pick blueberries there until we were caught by the prince's wardens. They would see us and break the pitchers we carried around our waists to hold the blueberries. As trespassers on private property, we weren't permitted to pick the blueberries. I don't know if it was because we were Jews or not. Nonetheless, we got away with this minor violation most of the time.

For many years, Prince Radziwill's pastures, sprinkled throughout the forest, had provided rich grazing for the livestock of Jewish farmers. In 1925, a decree was imposed stating that the pastureland could no longer be used by Jews. After years of fighting between Jews and the wardens, the prince eventually revoked the decree.

Our community also educated its youth. We attended Hebrew kindergarten and Hebrew school (*cheder*) and public school. Public school instructions were given in Polish, but we spoke Yiddish at home. For example, my name is Basia in Polish and Basi in Yiddish. Most Trochenbrod children completed school through the ninth grade, studying Polish, math, and some history. Although the administrators were Christian,

This is the Hebrew Day School in Trochenbrod in 1935.

the teachers were Jewish. Some young people would go on to gymnasium—high school—in a large city like Lutsk or Rovno. There was no high school in Trochenbrod. After graduation, many of the young men moved to the big city. Several of the boys attended *yeshiva,* a Hebrew religious school.

A portion of a child's education took place on the steps of our house. Neighbors would gather and talk about countries that I knew little or nothing about. I learned fascinating details about historical events and unusual places in the world. I would sit and listen to the adults discuss local politics or gossip. And on those steps we talked about America because many relatives lived there. We corresponded with our own overseas relations, mailing letters with pictures. Fortunately, the family photos that survived came from those we sent before the Holocaust, and pictures also exist because American relatives took photographs when they visited Trochenbrod before the Second World War.

I had a lot of close friends with whom I played. I think about them all of the time, at least as many as I can recall. I remember a girlfriend who wore glasses purchased in Lutsk. I was so impressed—she looked so sophisticated, so intelligent. I also played a lot with my girl cousins. Luckily, many of my cousins were my age because my aunts and uncles had babies at the same time.

Next door lived a deaf-mute child my age. I played with her all the time, and we communicated just fine. She taught me how to knit. Despite her condition, she was independent and socialized quite well. She was a normal, healthy child except that she couldn't hear or speak. I loved her and loved playing with her. She was a dear friend.

I remember all the fun at birthday parties. I remember getting a bobby pin or maybe a pressed flower or a piece of fancy paper at a birthday party for a present. To get a bobby pin for a birthday present was a big deal. Mothers would serve a little piece of cake and a small drink. That's how we celebrated our birthdays.

We didn't have games like the kids do today. We invented games using our imaginations. For example, we sometimes made our own dolls with towels. Today, this "trick" means a lot to my children and grandchildren. My parents and grandparents made dolls for me from towels, and I would do the same for my three sons. I gave birth to only boys so we didn't have dolls in our home, but I used to show my boys the kind of dolls I made as a child.

I would take a towel and fold it in such a way as to form the shape of a doll. Even though my boys were athletic and enjoyed typically boyish activities, they liked the dolls; however, they did not want me to use pink towels. Every now and then they would ask me, "Can you make me a doll?" As the years went by and these little boys grew into men and fathers, I made dolls for their children—my grandchildren. They, too, would say, "*Bubbe,* can you make us a doll?" Bubbe means "grandmother." They, too, loved the dolls.

Doll-making was a reminder of something that carried over from generation to generation, and my sons and their children love the dolls to this day. My family and friends sometimes ask me to make the doll for a child, and, of course, I gladly comply. It gives me as much joy to make these dolls as it does for those who receive them. It's such a unique creation compared to Barbie and other American girl dolls—perhaps that's why they like the dolls. Children are fascinated by the quick transformation of a piece of cloth to a doll.

Speaking of the word bubbe, my mother's father, Shiman, died when Mom was three, but I knew my other three grandparents well. I knew my mother's mother, Adel, and my father's parents. Later, when her husband Nusin died, Nechama, my father's mother, whom I called "Bubbe," moved in with us. As a matter of fact, my grandchildren call me that too. My boys and their spouses asked if that would be all right since I was the grandmother, or bubbe, of the grandkids. Of course I said yes. While growing up, my boys had called each of my parents Bubbe, and they wanted their kids to have a bubbe, too.

It's interesting to note how some Americans consider bubbe a derogatory term. They associate the word with an unflattering image of an old, Eastern European peasant woman who speaks broken English while wearing the often tattered head scarf known as a babushka. Yet to me, bubbe means only affection.

Unfortunately, it is a term that I don't think will be used much longer, except perhaps in Israel. Many Jewish people do not like the term, but I love it.

In addition to making dolls, another game I played I called "business," using wrappers from candy bars. We didn't have many candy wrappers, but if someone gave me a nickel, I would run to the store and buy candy. After eating the treat, I would save the wrappers and play "store." I would make up packages with sand or salt. Like the kids here who operate lemonade stands, I had business stands, selling a necklace, bead, or bobby pin. I became a businesswoman. I also liked the little playhouse we had. I enjoyed acting. Bernie and I, along with some other kids, put on small performances for other children.

At an early age I desired to achieve something. I was ambitious. I didn't know why I felt this way, but I knew I wouldn't be happy with the limited possibilities that existed in town. I felt a little different from the other girls, but I don't remember discussing "career choices" with anybody or asking any other girl what she wanted to be—I was not even ten yet. We ask kids today what they want to be when they grow up, but in those days girls did not have the same opportunities. I do believe that my dad, if he were alive today, would have encouraged and supported me to choose a profession that I would enjoy.

I respected and envied my mother for what she had accomplished in a little town and within her social circles and so forth. I didn't know then that housekeeping qualified as a job. Women did not work. They didn't work here either when I came to America. Even as a young girl, I felt some frustration, something that was missing that I needed to find. And it was the same way when I came here.

Had the Holocaust not happened, I think I would have left

Trochenbrod to go to a big city for an education and to accomplish something. I was ambitious and had dreams. I don't know what I could have done with my life, but I knew there was something better, something more in store for me.

Upon reflection, I suppose my desire to become more than a homemaker can be traced to my mother's independent nature, self-confidence, and intellectual interests. And from my father I learned the values of hard work, determination, and responsibility. My need to make something of myself, to achieve success in life, stemmed from my visits to Lutsk, a large city with a population close to forty thousand, about twenty miles southwest of Trochenbrod.

My father used to travel to Lutsk to buy accessories for his leather business: buckles, zippers, and forms for making shoes. He would bring me along occasionally—and what a thrill that was for me. All the kids back home envied me. Close friends of my parents lived in Lutsk, and Dad and I would stay with them.

We traveled there by horse and buggy. The person who brought the mail to town each day took people to and from Lutsk, picking up both mail and passengers. I do recall some people taking their own horse and buggies, traveling on the same road as we did. I didn't see a car until 1939, when an automobile drove into Trochenbrod. The driver must have been a man of importance. All the kids excitedly dashed toward the car.

Father took me to a photographer on one of these trips. He wasn't able to get the photograph right away, so he had to wait until his next visit to Lutsk. When he returned with my photograph, I remember him pulling out an envelope and, kiddingly, saying to others, "I want *zloty* [Polish currency] if

These two photographs are of the ribbon-cutting ceremony in 1939 for Trochenbrod's first paved street (above) and that same road today (below).

This is a studio photograph of me taken in Lutsk in the late 1930s just prior to the dramatic events that led to the Trochenbrod massacre.

you wish to look at Betty's picture." He thought his little girl was beautiful. Father made me feel pretty.

On another trip to Lutsk I watched several professional ballet dancers practicing in a courtyard. I sat and watched, mesmerized by their beauty, poise, and balance. I got to know them after a while. Once they asked me to bring them water for they were thirsty from practicing so strenuously, and I felt so honored to do something for them.

In Lutsk I remember also stopping in a gymnasium—a high school—and seeing older children in uniforms studying. Oh my God, did I want that! I knew that I wanted to be more than who I was. If I had been born in America with the opportunities that a young person has now, I think I would be either an attorney or an interior designer.

How did my siblings feel about their futures? I'm not sure about Shiman, the oldest. He was still in town working for my father even though he was old enough—at age seventeen in 1939—to have left Trochenbrod. I don't know if he expressed a desire to leave Trochenbrod or if my parents didn't allow him to leave. He went to public school and Hebrew school, but maybe he would have gone on to a higher learning institution, a *yeshiva*, or to a Jewish day school.

The peaceful life in Trochenbrod, however, was about to be shattered, permanently altering my ambitious dreams for the future, my education, my friendships with other children, my religious formation, and my relationship with family members. All this would occur as I neared the age of ten.

CHAPTER TWO

THE FOREST

＊In 1939, Poland fell into Soviet hands, and life in Trochenbrod abruptly changed. All businesses, including my father's leather shop, were confiscated. Shop owners now became managers, sacrificing income and profits to the shared wealth of communism. There were some Jews, however, who welcomed the communists: "I'm glad that the Soviets are in charge. They will take money from those who have too much money and spread it more equally among the rest of the people." Interestingly, when the communists left, these communist sympathizers were afraid to remain in Trochenbrod, frightened that they would be punished. They left town to live in the Soviet Union, some joining the Soviet military.

In school, students were indoctrinated in communism. We "comrades" wore red kerchiefs and pointed red caps, signaling our membership in the Soviet Young Pioneers, with the expectation of becoming patriots of Soviet communism. Each day in class we saluted and swore allegiance to the Soviet flag. We continued to study math and history, but the Russian language replaced Polish in the classroom.

No longer were the townspeople allowed to practice religion. All the synagogues were closed as were Christian churches outside of Trochenbrod. Religious observances were done secretly in various homes where men gathered to pray. Once Shiman was caught approaching a house to attend a prayer service. I don't recall what punishment, other than a stern warning, he was given. I do know that he never tried that again. Some of the Soviet officers may have chosen to overlook our efforts to maintain our religious practices, but we remained cautious, praying in secret. We were being watched; there were spies. Plain and simple, the communists considered people who practiced religion as anti-government and the enemy. Young people, whose minds, the communists thought, could be more easily molded by communist propaganda, were not allowed to pray or go to synagogue.

The people of Trochenbrod did not resist the takeover by the Soviets. Yes, soldiers and military equipment moved in,

In the far right corner of this 1932 photograph is my father holding me toward the camera, along with a large gathering of Trochenbroders.

but there was no violence, no spilling of blood. There was no organized resistance. What could we do anyway? They had an army, and we didn't. A general despondency descended on many Trochenbroders. Life seemed less cheerful. I don't remember a curfew, but they did stop business managers and workers from leaving the village in order to keep the village shops and services functioning.

Food was rationed. The community resented it, but expressing displeasure with this policy and/or others would not be wise, nor would it matter. People were afraid to speak up or were inclined to be apathetic because nothing could be changed. Protesting served no practical purpose.

Some Soviet soldiers settled in town, living in Jewish homes. There could be friendly moments between Soviet and Jew, and there were always bribes and political maneuvering. Some villagers befriended the Soviets to get better jobs. I remember a Jewish lady who lived with a Soviet officer. I don't know what she could benefit from this relationship; she couldn't gain anything politically.

It was assumed that the Soviet army had intended from the start of the occupation of Trochenbrod to force some of the men into their military. My father, who previously had served in the Polish army, was afraid that the Soviets would force him to be a soldier, so he devised a plan to escape recruitment.

My father asked me to pick dandelions and give them to him while he sat in the attic of our house. With my assistance, Dad then wrapped the dandelions around his arm with a bandage. Slowly, a few sores appeared. At the time, I didn't understand why Father was hurting himself in this manner.

I continued picking dandelions and applying more bandages to his arm. Eventually, the arm became visibly infected. It looked ugly. I learned later that to avoid becoming a soldier in the Soviet military, my father purposely damaged his arm. He believed that the Soviets would not take a man with an infection. As it turned out, none of the men were recruited into the military, so my dad's efforts at deceiving the Soviets were wasted. His arm, fortunately, healed on its own.

Although life in Trochenbrod under communist rule aroused anger, anxiety, and gloom, had we realized the terror that would follow, we would have joyfully accepted our situation with the Soviets.

I remember having a dream that there would be a war. I told my father the next morning about this dream, and, unfortunately, that dream came true that very same day.

The first airplane I saw made quite an impression. The aircraft was actually one of several that began dropping bombs on our town with no warning, beginning in July 1941. These were German bombers, which made clear that the Soviet Union and Germany were no longer allies. Reports had circulated that Germany had broken its alliance with the Soviet Union. We had known that the German army was getting closer and closer to Trochenbrod because we were the only family in Trochenbrod to own a radio. Radio broadcasts and refugees arriving from western Poland had told us about the German invasion, so we were somewhat prepared.

The bombers flew low as their engines screamed. Never was I so scared. The deafening sounds of exploding bombs and screeching aircraft compelled us to run for cover. Two townspeople were killed and several injured. Bernie's pet goat was killed. Ironically, I was both fascinated and frightened by the attack. These bombs were intended to obliterate buildings and people, and yet, in some way, I was awed by the spectacle of the unfolding drama.

In the next ten to fifteen minutes, the Nazi pilots continued to unload their bombs indiscriminately. There were no obvious military targets since Trochenbrod posed no threat to the Germans. Bombs exploded in gardens, yards, and on streets while our leather and glass factories were left untouched. Apparently the Nazis just wanted to let us know that they had arrived. So what if a few Jews were killed in the process?

Soon after the bombing, two German tanks, followed by soldiers, entered Trochenbrod. Immediately the commanding officer and his troops let us know how things were going to operate from this point on. Although they brought translators, we Jews understood the German language enough to follow their instructions. Right away they appointed several Jews as local administrators to work under their supervision; a Jewish council, called a *Judenrat* in German, was formed. I don't remember their choosing anybody from my immediate family.

During the Soviet occupation of Trochenbrod the tone was somber, but when the Germans arrived, the atmosphere was filled with apprehension and dread. We had heard rumors that Jews were being killed in other places, yet we didn't think these Germans would hurt us. Why would they harm a defenseless people who posed no threat? We were ordinary folks. It became clear that Jews in Trochenbrod and in other Nazi-occupied towns throughout Europe were living in a state of denial, unwilling to believe the potential depravity of their occupiers.

My father went back to his leatherworking shop, but no one went to school. When the Nazis came, everything stopped. Life changed drastically. Many were required to do forced labor, and many were ordered to pay hundreds of rubles to the Germans. Within three years, Trochenbrod went from Polish to Soviet to German control. Adapting to these drastic changes proved difficult for everyone and put most people on edge.

German officers appointed Ukrainians who lived outside of Trochenbrod as auxiliary police officers or *shutzmen*. The police worked with the Nazis to enforce German authority and rule. We were completely silenced, afraid to criticize any form of mistreatment. We had no choice but to follow the rules. What could we do otherwise? I don't ever remember seeing a Jew with a gun or a rifle. We had no means of fighting back. We were scared to death.

Although signs appeared that the population of Trochenbrod might be in physical danger, no one had been beaten or killed. I heard stories of men being taken out of town to work as slave labor, but the Germans took only a few. Those Jews who were removed, however, did not come back, an indication that things were going in the wrong direction.

Dad and others clearly suspected that the Nazis could harm the Jews of our town. Apparently, there was evidence that they had done so elsewhere, although we wouldn't find out until much later to what extent. Some villagers had even heard from refugees who had escaped from Krakow and Warsaw that Nazis were killing Jews and that they might kill us also. Father thought a hiding place might come in handy if the Nazis wanted to kill us. While the Germans occupied Trochenbrod, my father and a few others began to construct such a hiding place. Although I had vague notions that my father was building a secret shelter, I had never seen it. So as a kind of insurance policy, as a means to protect ourselves from any act of aggression, Father built a hideout.

No one except its builders knew the precise location or specific details of this secret room. They wanted to be certain that the Nazis would not discover this place, so Father and some other members of the family worked secretly. Children especially were kept in the dark regarding this enterprise because they might tell other children, who might in turn divulge the secret to adults. Always, always, the fear of betrayal loomed large during the Nazis' reign. The secret wall could hide only about a dozen people, so in an emergency there would not have been enough room for other Trochenbrod families, which was another reason for keeping the hiding place secret.

Behind our house stood a storage shed where Father kept wood, brooms, tools, and shovels. Using plywood, Dad built a wall across the back of the shed, matching its nine-foot width and eight-foot height. From the inside of the shed no one would suspect that the wall was anything other than the back wall, so expertly executed was the carpentry. The distance between the inner wall and the back of the shed was about three feet, just enough space in which to stand.

The day after I turned twelve, I was at home when I heard some disturbing noises outside. On the morning of August 11, 1942, the Nazis began knocking on doors, ordering all Trochenbrod villagers to leave our homes and walk, about two miles, to the center of town. They had prepared a designated area, a ghetto, for us to live in. At least, that is what we were told.

My grandmother Nechama, my father's mother, and I were alone in the front of the house when they ordered us to leave. I don't know where the rest of my family was. Perhaps they were hiding behind the wall already, or maybe they went to the hiding place afterwards. Maybe the Germans thought that my grandmother and I were the only people in the house at the time. I wasn't sure. I couldn't waste time contemplating the whereabouts of my other family members because the Nazis wanted us to leave immediately. We had no choice but to follow orders—immediately.

The Germans allowed us to bring some basic necessities; we did not suspect that we were about to become participants in the "final solution" to the Jewish problem. My grandmother and I, along with hundreds of other Jews, proceeded to walk to the ghetto. As I walked I thought of my family again. Where were Father, Mother, Shiman, and Bernie? I initially concluded that they were probably following somewhere behind us.

When we reached the center of town and after a couple of hours of sitting and waiting for my parents and siblings to arrive, I began to wonder why they were taking so long to join us. I grew increasingly suspicious of the situation that the several thousands who had now gathered were facing. I sensed danger. I sensed death.

After asking my grandmother to watch the bundles of belongings that we brought from home, without any hesitation, I sprinted toward home. Some voice inside me told me that my family must be hiding at home. I had no doubt whatsoever. I later realized that my foolhardy attempt to escape the ghetto might have resulted in my being shot.

I was the only person moving in the opposite direction. At one point on my mad dash, I darted between the legs of a German soldier. He was looking elsewhere and was momentarily distracted, but my small stature helped me to wriggle through somehow.

When I reached my house, I began a search for my family. I looked up and down to no avail. Then I remembered the secret wall allegedly located in the shed. I didn't remember where it was exactly; I knew only very little about the project. Before the Nazis began knocking on doors, we did not discuss an emergency plan.

I was certain that my family was not in the house, and that's when I walked to the shed, located just a few feet behind the house. I stepped in and stood in the middle, unaware and even doubtful of the existence of a secret wall. I began talking, identifying myself: "I am Betty. I know you have a hiding wall here. And you didn't come to the ghetto and I got scared. I got scared looking for you. So please let me in." No sounds. I became more desperate, my voice rising with every syllable. I was now yelling rather than talking.

Because I couldn't find the wall—since my father had seamlessly blended it into the structure of the shed—my frustration mounted. All the walls appeared identical. I couldn't see the secret wall. Maybe, there was no wall, I thought. Maybe my family is hiding in a hole under the ground instead. My urgent pleas over the next few minutes went ignored.

I then began to think that they didn't want to let me in because maybe they thought that someone—a soldier or a collaborator—may have followed me. Perhaps they believed that another Jew or several wanted to hide behind the wall with our family. My pleas intensified and I began to scream and cry that I also wanted to live, that no one had followed me: "I'm here alone! Please, please let me in!"

Finally, near the corner of the back wall, a tiny door opened, revealing a very narrow opening, just large enough to crawl into. An arm—brother Shiman's—emerged and pulled me in. There was a secret wall after all!

Pictured here is the extended Potash family in 1933 with Shiman, Bernie, and me in the front while Mother and Father stand in the back row.

In the cramped space stood sixteen terrified individuals: the five Potashes; another family of five, my adult and younger cousins; three more cousins; an orphan boy, a friend of Bernie's; and a married couple who were friends of the family. We were six adults and ten young people in total. We could only stand since the small dimensions of the hiding place would not allow much movement. My father had stored some provisions inside the wall, burlap bags filled with potatoes and bread, enough food for several days. Despite the darkness of the hideout, we could see a little bit of the outside through several cracks inside the shed. Inside the wall, Father demanded that no one talk, sneeze, cry, or make a sound. As we were within hearing distance of the Nazi patrols, we had to be perfectly quiet and still to remain alive.

After forcing most of Trochenbrod's Jews to walk toward the ghetto, soldiers and collaborators went from door to door, looking for those who might be hiding or who had refused to march into town. From the shed we could see the Nazis and their henchmen picking up little children and roughly hoisting them (sometimes by the hair) onto a truck to be driven away.

A few moments later, we saw my grandmother Adel, who lived across the street from us, being forcibly pulled from her house. She must have become suspicious of the motives behind the establishment of the so-called "ghetto" and decided to hide in her home. They shot her dead in the courtyard a few feet from her front door. We now began to grasp the full significance of the plans the Nazis had made for those marshaled into town.

We stayed motionless throughout the morning and into the late afternoon, when rapid machine-gun fire interrupted the stillness, shattering our nerves and our hearts. We eventually would ascertain the source of those blasts. We were about to learn the full extent of man's incomprehensible capacity for evil.

Approximately a mile from where we were hiding, about 4,500 Jews were being systematically murdered. We found out that all the Jews who walked to the ghetto would later be transferred two miles by truck to an area next to Yaromel Forest. Here, after they were ordered to undress, they were shot and their bodies fell into prepared trenches. The Trochenbrod Massacre had just been carried out.

And because I understood that my grandmother Nechama was among those murdered, I still live with the guilt of leaving her behind as I ran out of the ghetto. I knew that Grandmother couldn't run as I could because she was old and frail, but maybe I could have done something to save her life. To honor her memory along with the memory of all those killed, I light a candle each year on the anniversary of their deaths.

We thought that some of the Nazis had stationed themselves in our house, so now more than ever, all of us behind the wall had to remain perfectly quiet. Our lives depended on our silence. Among the sixteen of us was a toddler about a year-and-a-half old. At one point the girl began screaming, and the mother could not hush her child's cries. Tragically, in the process of silencing her daughter, the mother suffocated her, afraid that her other two children and the rest of us, for that matter, would be discovered by the Nazis. The dead child was wrapped in burlap. We hoped to give her a decent burial when the situation was less dangerous, when we could emerge from our hiding place. Sixteen became fifteen.

Believing that it was safe to leave our hiding spot, during the middle of the night we squirmed out of the wall and headed toward nearby Radziwill Forest. We were blessed with a rainstorm, which muffled the sounds of our movements. One by one, we got down on our hands and knees and crawled through a drainage ditch in our garden until it seemed safe to stand up. The ditches guided us to the edge of the woods.

Little did we suspect that these woods would be our home for so long!

We brought basically nothing to the forest except the clothes we wore, and we were rescued later wearing those same clothes, when they were nothing more than shreds. In the woods, we made "shoes" from trees by wrapping the white bark around our feet.

Here I am in my beautiful apartment as I retrace memories of almost seventy years ago. When I'm cold, I simply turn up the thermostat to make it warmer. And now I think of all the people who froze to death during the Holocaust, hiding in the forest and hills. How did my family survive? We had frozen fingers and frozen toes. To this day, I still require shots in two of my toes every now and then to stop the pain.

My father had devised another survival option after he had built the wall—bunkers. Earlier in the Nazi occupation and, fortunately, sensing the sinister intentions of the German army, Dad and his cousins had dug two large bunkers, three miles apart, about two miles inside the forest. These bunkers—covered by fallen trees, branches, leaves, and soil—were hidden from view. The entrance was a small opening, about the size of a pillow. The bunkers resembled small caves, and were long enough to allow only about a dozen people to lie down next to each other and deep enough to sit in. We slept so close to each other that I felt like a sardine in a can after I crawled in.

A few German soldiers stayed in the town for a brief period to make sure that all the Jews had been killed or to look for some who may have escaped. But most of the Germans stayed in Lutsk. The Germans rarely visited the woods to search for those who escaped. They employed, instead, Ukrainian collaborators to do their work because these men knew the forest much better than the Nazis did. Another reason that the Nazis recruited Ukrainians to do most of the dirty work was because the additional manpower—ten Ukrainian guards for every German soldier—saved German resources.

Some say that Ukrainian nationalism, a long-standing hatred for the Jews, or a genuine fear of reprisals from the

Nazis motivated many Ukrainians to assist in these heinous actions. I'm not sure what incentives drove these Ukrainians to become Nazi enforcers, but the threat of being detected and subsequently caught haunted us daily. A farmer might notice one of our heads peeking up or hear one of us talking or maybe spot our bunker. If someone detected our presence, he or she would likely report our location to the Nazis, who would then begin a search.

Fiercely nationalistic, Ukrainians resented any occupiers on their land, which was considered the most fertile in all of Europe, whether the occupiers were Polish, Soviet, or German. Tensions between Ukrainians and Jews are well documented. Some Ukrainians believe that several Bolshevik Jews played key roles in the starvation deaths of five to seven million Ukrainians from 1932 to 1933—the Holodomor—by means of a forced famine under Stalin's regime.

Before I go any further, I must point out that not all Ukrainians were Nazi sympathizers. True, the Germans, upon their arrival in Trochenbrod, did appoint Ukrainians as auxiliary police officers or *shutzmen*. And many of these Ukrainians did commit terrible acts of cruelty toward the Jews at this time, here and in the neighboring villages of Lozisht and Klubochyn. However, many Jews were rescued from death by Ukrainians who risked their own lives to hide them. It must be remembered that hundreds of Ukrainians from Klubochyn, assisting a Jewish resistance group in Trochenbrod who took up military action against the Nazis, were executed for helping the Jews.

Unfortunately, the majority of Ukrainians and Poles tended to be passive and refused to act in defense of the Jews, who were beginning to be openly murdered in large numbers.

Much more serious than battling weather conditions and informants, however, were the challenges in finding food. Since the weather in late summer and early fall was warm, we could eat blueberries. Occasionally, farms provided beets, cabbages, and carrots, but soon we exhausted the supply. Another source of food came from the orchards. For a little while at least we could pick up fruit from the ground, which helped sustain us.

My father was our group's leader. He was the oldest, wisest, and most practical. We could not have survived without his guidance and decision-making. One decision that he made early on was to send me, his youngest child, on scavenger hunts for food.

As colder weather approached, Father decided to send his little girl, now twelve, out at night, alone, to search for food. He believed my small size would make it less likely for me to be spotted. Yes, I'm sure that he knew the risks and worried enormously, but he thought this strategy to be worth the potential hazards.

Another reason that Dad chose me to scavenge for food is because he had two sons who were circumcised. If they were captured by the enemy, they could easily be identified as Jews.

Surrounding Radziwill Forest were farms owned by Ukrainians and Poles. A couple of times a week, I left the bunker and walked about two miles to these farms. The flickering lights from the farms helped to guide me. I wouldn't get lost on my way back to the bunker because I already memorized the route from seeing the area during daylight. I was scared, but I was familiar with the area. I was careful to remain as quiet as I possibly could, and often crawled rather than walked.

Sometimes before crossing a road I would see a couple of Nazis on motorcycles. I would lie flat on the ground or hide under a bush or behind a tree at these times. I was regularly running way from noises like an approaching car or motorcycle. Any sound would alarm me. Although my duties took place mostly at night, I sometimes left in the twilight to make it easier for me to see. Drainage ditches provided effective places in which to hide.

I often considered the possibility of a farmer catching me on his property. What would have happened? Would he have turned me over to the Nazis? Or would he have rescued me?

When I arrived at a farm, I would look for a trash can and reach inside. If I could find anything in the garbage that felt like food, I took it. I wore a piece of burlap wrapped around my shoulder, and put what I discovered in there. Sometimes I found half a potato thrown away with its peelings, a piece of cooked meat, lard, vegetables, or fruit. I couldn't see clearly in the pitch darkness of night, and whatever I thought might be food, despite its slimy texture and smelly scent, I grabbed. I wasn't concerned about the food being spoiled. I learned firsthand the truth of the maxim "You'll eat just about anything when you're hungry." Sometimes I took what felt like a piece of cooked meat or a bone or an apple.

I also hunted for food in barns, sometimes finding wheat or flour, which we would mix with water when I returned to the bunker. On good days I brought back beets, beans, radishes, and cucumbers that had not yet been pulled from the soil or had been discarded because of rot.

Whatever I returned with was rationed by my father. Let's say that I brought back half a loaf of stale bread or a boiled potato or an apple or a piece of lard. Since my orthodox father would never eat meat that was not kosher, it broke my heart to watch him, forced by hunger, to eat a piece of lard. This was the only time in his life that he compromised his principles, his faith, and you could see how it pained him. Dad would take it and cut it into little pieces and hand to each person a piece and save the rest in a cloth. Everyone got a little bit. Father permitted us to eat once a day.

Dad brought to the forest a tiny square stove, the size of a dinner plate. On this stove we would, on very rare occasions, cook potato peelings. In the warmer months we were less concerned with starting a fire than in the winter. Building a fire in the winter would have been foolish because our location would have been spotted quickly.

We were lucky because my dad's Christian friend, Jusef, a local Polish farmer who had often bought goods from Father's shop—and the only person outside of our group who knew the location of the bunkers—would visit us every couple of weeks. Jusef risked his life, and his own family's as well, to see us. He had to be careful not to be seen by the Nazi collaborators. Had they found out that Jusef was helping us, surely he would have been killed, and, of course, our whereabouts would have been discovered. He kept us informed as to what was going on in the village and surrounding area. Jusef would also bring some food—bread, apples, and, once, hard-boiled eggs—to ease our hunger. We were hoping that one day he would come to tell us that the war was over and that we could leave the woods. Without Jusef's assistance during this time, I doubt that we would have survived. He was a trusted friend.

There were no toilets, obviously, so one went to the bathroom, preferably at night, to avoid being detected by our enemies. Personal hygiene was not a priority, so we became accustomed to body odors and eventually lice. Occasionally we'd find a puddle deep enough to wash up in. The rancid food and vile sanitary conditions induced a variety of ailments, including vomiting, diarrhea, and stomach pains. I can trace the origins of my stomach's sensitivity today to my digestive habits in the forest.

After hiding in the woods for several weeks, Jusef told us that some Jews who had escaped the massacre by hiding in houses or in the forest had returned to town. The few Germans who remained near Trochenbrod seemed, curiously, to have ignored these survivors. Perhaps these Jews were being used as slave labor.

That evening, we gathered to discuss the possibility of going back to the village. With winter on the horizon, nights becoming increasingly colder, and the likelihood that food and water would continue to become scarce, we agreed to take a chance and head back.

Our destination that night was two houses on the outskirts of town. Here, from Jusef's reports, might be a soup kitchen or a shelter. Unbelievably, we got lost even though we were only a few miles from our bunker in the forest. We learned that we had walked in circles. My parents were lifelong Trochenbroders and knew their way around for hundreds of miles, yet that night, we got lost.

Exhausted from our hike, Father told us to climb into a ditch. The plan was to wait until daybreak and then resume the search for the two houses. Minutes later, while sitting in the ditch, we heard gunfire. The shots came from those two houses, where about fifty Jews had been murdered. Another killing spree had started.

After the Nazi killed these Jews, they burned Trochenbrod to the ground. We saw the flames as we ran away to the second bunker in the woods. Because we thought that someone might have discovered the first bunker during our absence, we turned around and headed back to the forest. And that's where we would live for the next year, moving from one bunker to the other.

One member of our group left us around this time. Brother Shiman departed to live in another bunker in the forest to help some cousins who desperately needed a leader. He would be missed, but we believed, as did the members of the other bunker, that making Shiman the head of their group was a wise decision.

In late September 1942, with Yom Kippur approaching, Jusef told us that the Nazis were no longer visiting Trochenbrod. Why would they? There were probably no factories left nor a living soul or a house. According to Jusef, the Germans kept an office in the nearest town, Kivritz, outside of Trochenbrod. My father decided it was now safe to return.

Sketchy rumors persisted that the Nazis needed workers for one of the remaining glass factories. Slave labor would be much better than our current state of affairs, we thought.

Just about every Jew—agnostic, reformed, conservative, or orthodox—prays and fasts on Yom Kippur. Of course, the fasting wouldn't be difficult as we became quite accustomed to not eating. So we decided to go back to town, a couple of days before the holy day, even though we expected to see few buildings, if any, remaining after the fire, hoping that other Jews would come out of hiding and do the same thing. And sure enough, about a hundred Jews showed up.

We all looked like monkeys, like the walking dead, like skeletons, with no shoes, ripped clothing, and haggard expressions. We embraced, kissed, and wept. We were overcome with joy because we didn't know others had survived.

Someone built a fire and somebody else found some beans. We cooked a pot of beans, pretending it was chicken soup. We ate the beans right out of the pot and, using our hands, slurped the broth from the beans. Everyone took a little bit of soup from the pot with their hands after it had cooled. We had not eaten this well in over a year.

We stayed there for a little while in two houses on the outskirts of town. Yom Kippur arrived and everyone rose in the morning to pray. But we awakened to a very clever ploy by the Nazis. They had come to join us, but not in prayer. They had surrounded the homes, knowing that if people were hiding somewhere, they would gather together to come and pray on this day. They must have gotten word from an informant.

We were instructed to open all of the windows and doors and told to run. Adults began throwing children out of windows, and some of these kids ran into the woods. We knew that if we didn't run, the Nazis would gather us together like they did in the ghetto. There was at least a chance some could survive. If we were to survive, my father had said that we would meet in the forest at a designated place.

So we ran for our lives.

Bullets rained down. Amid rifle shots I stumbled over corpses of adults and children, including the bodies of several cousins and an uncle, whose throat was slashed. Another Trochenbrod massacre had taken place. My adult cousin, who had suffocated her toddler, and her husband escaped, but their two sons were killed. The fourteen in our party at the beginning of that morning had shrunk to seven after the surprise attack.

As we gathered at our bunker in the woods to mourn the loss of more of our loved ones, somehow Father managed to keep us from falling into complete despair. His resilience in the face of hopelessness kept us alive. He firmly stuck to a plan that he believed would keep us safe and ultimately would lead to our freedom.

As the evenings got colder and colder, I continued scavenging for food. Despite the little food that I found and my father's rationing system, the group grew increasingly desperate, hungry, and cold. We were growing weaker and more miserable by the minute.

On one occasion I found some loaves of bread at a farm I visited. It was a miracle, a godsend. I seized the bounty and scampered back to the bunker. Everyone's eyes bulged. My father said, "The bread will have to last us for a couple of weeks. My little girl won't have to risk her life for a couple of weeks." He cut a little piece and each day he gave each person a little piece.

He stored the bread on a little shelf, and my space was near the bread. The next night I was sitting near the bread and thought to myself, *What the heck, I deserve a little extra since I'm the one who went out and found the treasure.* I proceeded to poke a hole in one of the loaves. I wasn't satisfied with one poke, so I poked another hole. After eating the bread I felt so guilty and miserable.

The next morning my father noticed two holes in the bread and said that besides all the misery, cold, and lice, now we had rats. What could we do? "The rats are lucky we didn't find them," Father stated. I said to myself that they don't know that I'm the rat.

The next night I did the same thing. That's it. I promised myself I would not do it again. I felt so awful. The following morning my father looked around and said maybe we should eat the bread before the rats do because now we have two more holes in the bread. I felt terrible. A guilty look spread over my face. My eyes grew larger. He stared at me, and his eyes caught mine and then he made an announcement. He knew his little girl. He said, "I think I found the rat." He moved me from one end of the bunker to the other. The loaves of bread were safe for as long as they lasted.

While the supply of bread was running out, the winter weather made it impossible for me to continue my visits to the neighboring farms. I would have left footprints in the snow, and, like everyone else, I was weakened by the cruel temperatures and hunger. At this point, we stayed close to our bunker to avoid the risk of being found. Huddling together provided warmth. The snow was useful, however, in two distinct ways. Putting our heads in the snow froze the lice on our heads, and the snow provided our drinking water.

Hunger is the worst pain in the world. I have given birth and had serious surgeries, but never have I experienced anything close to the pain of hunger. In the forest, we obsessed over food, thought constantly of food. Eating that small piece of bread that Father had set aside for the only meal of the day was the only thing on our minds. Food was all we thought about.

I was so hungry at times that I ate clover and drank blood. Often, we would eat something and throw up or get sick, but swallowing anything was comforting.

Watching Mother and Father suffer through this period saddened me. What grieved me the most was seeing the sorrow in their eyes at they observed how hungry we children were. They hated to see us suffer. They always gave us more food than they took themselves. In fact, many times Mom and Dad would give us their portions.

Brother Bernie and I used to play a game where we would ask each other the question: "What would you eat if you were able to choose?" Bernie would answer, "Bread." I would answer, "Soup." My father did not find this game as amusing as we did, so he ordered us to stop. Dad thought that it was not appropriate to find humor in so desperate a time.

I don't know how we survived. We resembled skeletons, and yet no one died, proving that you can live on very little food. Maybe it was God's will. Maybe it was a miracle. Or was it luck, chance, or fate that saved us? If you are a great believer, you may say that God wanted us to live. I've always said that we survived through chance.

One day in December, the kind and courageous Jusef informed us that he heard in town that we had been discovered and that the Nazis were coming to kill us that afternoon. We must run away immediately, he insisted.

It was now winter and treacherously cold, and we didn't know where to hide or escape. We didn't have a third bunker to go to. And that's when my father remembered a bunker that he had visited where eleven Jews were hiding. Perhaps we could go and hide with them. But after walking the mile to this other bunker and taking a look at its size, we concluded that this cave could not hold one additional person, let alone seven.

So suicide became a very attractive option. We had no other choice since we had nowhere to go, nowhere to hide. We couldn't stand outside; we'd suffer even more by freezing to death. We agreed to go back to the cave and wait for the Nazis to come and shoot us dead. This was a mutual decision, not only my father's.

While waiting, my father instructed us that when the soldiers came to kill us, we should not just stand there and get killed, but that we should run. This was for two reasons: some may survive, and, if so, we could meet at a designated place; and, more importantly, when Nazis and collaborators found Jews hiding in the forest, they didn't just shoot them, they tortured them first before they killed them. We saw evidence of this monstrous brutality in the forest. We saw a woman's breast after it was sliced off. We saw stomachs, tongues, ears, and fingers on the ground. We saw hanging bodies. We saw dismembered bodies. In the darkness of night we would bury these remains.

After witnessing these atrocities, we understood perfectly Father's recommendation that we run when the Nazis found us.

At our bunker everybody hugged each other as we said our good-byes. Mom and Dad embraced. We all agreed that we would meet in heaven because we already had endured our hell on earth. Interestingly, I didn't see expressions of fear on the faces before me. Perhaps we had become so accustomed to pain and suffering, both physical and mental, that we had lost our will to survive.

So we waited and waited, and finally, we heard footsteps outside the bunker. Death was about to pay us a visit. My father told Bernie, who was near the entrance, to see who was there, as though we didn't already know. Everyone was wondering why Bernie was smirking when he turned around. We believed that he had simply gone crazy at the sight of the Nazis, knowing we would die soon. Well, as it turned out, Bernie was smiling because, instead of the Nazis, it was Jusef! There was an error in the Christian's report. The Nazis slaughtered the eleven Jews in the other bunker, not us. If these unfortunate people had found room in their bunker for us, I wouldn't be here to tell this story.

Hungry, dirty, and exhausted, we clung to our bleak lives, and our previous lives in Trochenbrod seemed to be more dream than reality. Since the murder of the eleven Jews in the other bunker, we were certain that we would be discovered soon. Our luck had to run out.

The seven of us found our next lodging in a marsh inside the forest because Father decided that there was no place for us to hide anymore. Our bunkers were no longer secure, so my father came up with the idea of living in a marsh. "You know, there's a big marsh in the forest." He didn't think that "the Nazis would wish to dirty their beautiful uniforms looking for dirty Jews there." Our town no longer existed—we couldn't go there. We lost contact with Jusef. We didn't know ahead of time that we were going into the swamp, so Jusef didn't know where we had gone.

Living in the marsh made it more difficult for me to scavenge for food. I would go up to the villages at night and see blinking lights, but returning to the marsh was so confusing that it was nearly impossible for me to find my way back. The knee-deep mud, thick vegetation, and putrid water made travel difficult. I still had a burlap sack tied around me, and I would go into barns and garbage containers. Sometimes an orchard would have frozen fruit on the ground from the previous year. I took anything that I could gather. But coming back was very hard because I didn't always know in which direction to go, so we set up a signal. I would clap three times when I was near our hideout. My family would clap back to me, and I would follow the sound to help me find my way to them.

We built a small bridge from fallen trees and twigs and leaves about three or four feet above the water. That's where we lived. We weren't as well hidden as we were in the forest bunkers, but we didn't think that anyone would bother to look for us in so desolate an area. We would have preferred the bunker instead of living in the misery of the muck and water. We lived in the marsh for a couple of months, looking more and more like wild animals. I told my dad at this time not to worry about anyone hurting us because if someone did see us, "they would be frightened and run away from our scary appearances."

One of the lighter moments involved a beautiful black snake that inhabited the marsh. The water snake became our pet. We weren't afraid of the snake. Coming and going, going and coming, it entertained us while distracting us momentarily from our misery. As hungry as we were, the snake was lucky that we didn't eat it. I don't know why we didn't. Maybe we thought it was poisonous.

But most of the time we wondered how much longer could we hold on.

CHAPTER THREE

EXODUS

✳ On a warm late summer morning in 1943, while living in the marsh, Father said he was going to take us on a "field trip." We just rolled our eyes. What kind of field trip could he be talking about here in this dreary place? He said, "On this beautiful sunny day we will go to the edge of the forest. Maybe we'll see humanity. Maybe we'll see some animals." Wearing the same clothes for nearly a year, barefoot, hungry, and depressed, we seven began our walk.

We chose our vantage point just behind a row of trees to avoid being seen. We peered through the branches of leaves at the sunlit pasture. What a treat it was to see farmers and their wives with their children frolicking about, horses, cows, and chickens.

I stared and stared, wishing that I were one of those farm animals who roamed freely. I wished I were one of those birds who flew above the farm so that I could fly away from all my troubles.

After relishing the rustic scene for about ten minutes, Father said that we could stay a bit longer. We knew that we risked the chance of being seen each moment we lingered. I had visited these Christian farms, situated in Polish and Ukrainian hamlets near Trochenbrod, at night while scavenging for food. Some of those who lived here could very well be collaborators.

As we continued to absorb and envy the idyllic scene, Bernie eagerly pointed to something in the distance and said, "Oh my God, take a look, take a look!" He had spied an apple orchard. "I'm going to pick some fruit; there must be some apples on the ground." So, before any of us could stop him, Bernie took off and ran. In a minute or so we saw Bernie picking up some apples from the ground. We prayed that no one would discover him.

Suddenly, three horses appeared. Riding atop those horses were three uniformed soldiers armed with rifles. They charged after Bernie, picked him up, and put him on a horse. The Nazis had captured Bernie. That is, we assumed they were Germans.

From our location behind the trees we saw the soldiers asking Bernie questions. He was obviously frightened. I'm sure my terrified brother told them all about himself and us. Bernie must have told them where we were hiding because the soldiers quickly turned toward us. We were about to be apprehended and probably tortured and killed. As the horses galloped in our direction, we ran for our lives. We soon learned how much faster horses are than people as we were swiftly surrounded.

As they came closer we were both startled and relieved to learn that these soldiers were not German. They were partisans, members of the Soviet underground, a resistance movement designed to disrupt the Eastern Front of the German army. Modeled on the Red Army, the partisans wore Soviet uniforms with red insignias.

They smiled at us, and we smiled back. We were saved. Could this nightmare of the past year be coming to a close?

They took us with them, and we walked alongside for a short distance to their camp in the forest, where we met up with a couple of dozen soldiers. We went inside a tent and were asked questions. We knew enough Russian to answer their questions since Trochenbrod was recently occupied by the Soviet Union, and we had attended a Soviet school.

They assigned my mother a post as a cook, and I assisted her. Mother and I peeled countless potatoes. We were useful to the partisans as workers. At first they didn't have much food and clothing to give us. But when the partisans left at night on their missions to blow up roads, buildings, bridges, and trains, they would go into homes and demand food, clothing, and other supplies and provisions, and bring these items back and share the spoils with us.

The war was still on, but we felt safer under their protection. We were constantly on the move, setting up camp in one place and then another to avoid being discovered by the Nazis. Since we were quite weak, the constant walking exhausted us. The muddy terrain—there were no roads—added to the difficulty of these marches. Occasionally, however, the soldiers would be kind and hoist my mother or me onto a horse, temporarily alleviating our fatigue.

It was at this time that we were reunited with Shiman. My oldest brother, now twenty, six feet tall, and a grown man, had become an official partisan, complete with rifle and uniform. This was the last time we would see Shiman, who eventually would leave the camp to join other partisans on the Soviet war front.

While my mother and I remained at the campsites to cook meals, Father and Shiman accompanied the partisans on their exploits. Dad never told me exactly what his role was on these assignments. Bernie, only fifteen, provided menial labor like finding firewood and gathering food and supplies.

The Soviet partisans seemed confident that they were going to win the war. They sometimes would provide optimistic reports about how well the Red Army was succeeding against the German military forces on the front.

While we stayed with the partisans, we asked how Jews were being treated in other parts of Poland and the Soviet Union. We were not told of other Trochenbrod massacres, but we did learn, although vaguely, of widespread Nazi mistreatment against Jews. But it wouldn't be until the end of 1944 when we would learn, along with the rest of the world, the full magnitude and horrors of Auschwitz and other death camps.

I'll never forget the day when we were brought to the forest to assist in the torture and murder of a Nazi collaborator, a Ukrainian. Apparently this individual had not only been an informant but one who had himself tortured a Jew. The partisans started a fire under a four-legged bathtub and then filled it with water. When the water reached the boiling point, they placed the terrified man into the tub and demanded that we watch.

I tried to look elsewhere, but one of the partisans grabbed my neck and turned my head toward the anguished victim and shouted to every Jew in the audience: "This man and others like him butchered your family members and you are afraid to look? What's the matter with you? Here's a chance at revenge!" I can still hear the prisoner's screams to this day.

As I shook with fear and revulsion at this hideous sight, some Jews stepped forward and began to strike the Ukrainian with branches, feverishly exclaiming, "Murderer! This is for my mother! This is for my father! This is for my brother! This is for my sister! This is for my child!"

After about five months, in the spring of 1944, the partisans and the war dictated that we should be sent elsewhere. The partisans couldn't take two young kids and a mother with them on their latest assignment, so Mother, Bernie, and I were transferred by train to a collective farm to pick potatoes for the soldiers. They sent my father by train to Kiev to work in a leather factory. The remaining members of our group were sent to other Soviet destinations.

Although our living conditions were a dramatic improvement—we were given food and shelter—over those in the forest, we lived like refugees. Initially we all got sick from eating because our stomachs couldn't digest even the paltry amounts of additional food we were taking in. In addition to the vomiting and diarrhea, we suffered from a wide range of maladies, including bleeding ulcers and boils. Some of us needed medical attention. It took a long time for our bodies to adjust to a semi-normal diet.

At the collective, each person received one potato per day. Twenty-five people lived in one house with one little stove, and we worked twelve to fourteen hours a day picking potatoes. Incredibly, I still love potatoes today. When the time came to stand in line to cook our potatoes, we were so tired that sometimes we couldn't eat. We would fall asleep from exhaustion, but it was better than living in the woods or the swamp—at least we felt relatively safe. No one was coming after us. The only danger came from the bombs and planes and artillery fire, signs that the war was still on.

It was at this time that my mother suggested that I, now thirteen, travel alone to Kiev, about two hundred miles away, to find my father. She had hoped that my father could come back with me to the collective so that we would be a family again. I suppose she felt confident that I could handle the challenge of such a journey based on my experiences in scavenging for food from neighboring farms.

The next day, wearing my little red-pointed cap that assured the authorities I was a Soviet partisan, a Young Pioneer, I walked toward the nearby railroad station, carrying a little bundle that I tied around my waist. My provisions included bread, hard-boiled eggs, and an apple. I didn't think that I needed a ticket. Because of the war, everything, including train transportation, was disrupted. There really was no organized government. I thought that they would see my hat and simply allow me on the train, but no such luck. Either the officials didn't want to be responsible for my safety or simply didn't want me on the train, I'm not sure. The cars were packed with soldiers so perhaps there were no seats available.

Neither my mother nor I had any clue as to what I was getting myself into. What guarantee did I have that I would find Dad in such a large city? If I found him, would he be permitted to return anyway? How would I find food and water? Where would I stay and sleep? Another obstacle would be the fact that a war was going on and many railroad tracks were bombed, so people had to switch trains often, after a hundred miles or less. In other words, would I be able to arrive safely in Kiev?

Since I couldn't have a seat on the train, I foolishly chose to sit on the outside steps of a railroad car, tightly gripping the two handrails as the train moved out of the station. No one saw me. I had become quite adept in the last year in staying hidden from view. Even the soldiers inside didn't realize I was sitting outside. I'm certain that they wouldn't have let me ride outside if they had seen me.

I desperately gripped the handrails alongside the steps, knowing that if I let go, I'd likely fall off the speeding train to my death. A strong wind began to whip my face, bruising and numbing it. However, my hands ached much more than my face. I soon regretted my decision to find a seat on the outside of the cars, but I did not dare to let go. I had to go as far as the train went because I couldn't jump off. After a few hours the train stopped because we came upon tracks that had been destroyed by explosives. I got off the train along with the other passengers and waited for another train to arrive.

Miraculously, my red hat stayed on.

When the second train pulled up, I chose a less hazardous place to sit. Attached to the passenger cars were cattle cars. I hopped aboard one of these cars, sharing the compartment with cows and the men who took care of them, and rode all the way to Kiev.

I eventually reached Kiev in a couple of days. It was a vast city with gorgeous parks. I started walking the streets, intending to stop at every building with a red flag since I believed my father was employed at a governmental business.

I started asking people where I might find my father. I asked where I could find the military leather factory where my father, I believed, worked as a partisan. I took along a little picture of my father and showed it to many strangers. No one I met recognized Dad, and no one knew of a leather factory. I doggedly continued my search, roaming from street to street and building to building. I didn't doubt, on this first day in Kiev, that I would find my father. At the end of the day and after eating my last bit of food, I found a park, where I eventually slept that night.

On the second day, I awoke, brushed myself off, and started walking again from building to building. Again, no one knew anything of my father's whereabouts. Having finished the food the evening before and beginning to feel extremely hungry, I started begging for food. Fortunately, people gave me some food and water, which helped to sustain me. One kind woman gave me something to eat and a cup of tea. She said I could keep the cup, which made it easier for me to keep a supply of water with me whenever I found some. I wish I still had this cup as a keepsake of her generosity. At the end of day two, weary and hungry and losing hope that I'd find Father, I again slept in the park.

On the third day, I thought to myself that this would be my final day in Kiev. I had little strength left to wander aimlessly around a city I was unfamiliar with. I was a small child who was worn out physically and emotionally. But something inside drove me to continue my search for Dad, so I resumed my strategy of walking, asking questions, and knocking on doors. I decided that if I failed in my efforts, then I would return to the train station and, ultimately, to Mom, Bernie, and the collective farm.

Late in the afternoon on the third day, I lost hope of ever finding my father. I went back to the park and decided I would sleep there and leave Kiev the next morning. I sat down on a bench when a stranger walked over, sat next to me, and began to ask questions: "Little girl, what are you doing here? Why are you in the park?" Today, you would be afraid of a stranger asking questions. At that time, I wasn't afraid of anyone—I didn't care.

I began telling him my long story, explaining that I came here to look for my father. I then began to describe my father in greater detail. At this moment, I began to weep. I felt so discouraged that I had not accomplished what I intended to do. I became depressed and upset at the thought of going back to the collective farm empty-handed.

After patiently listening to my travails, the man began asking me questions. I explained that my father was in the leather business and he was sent from our partisan camp to work in a military leather factory. When I finished providing these details, he said, "Give me your hand, little girl, and come with me." I gave him my hand and left the park bench with him. He didn't tell me where he was taking me. I thought perhaps he was taking me to a house where I would be given soup or something else to eat. Or maybe he would find a bed for me to sleep in.

Instead he escorted me to a leather factory—only three hundred feet away—where my father worked! God had sent me an angel! This must be a miracle. When I walked inside the building, I ran toward Father, who picked me up and wouldn't put me down as he spun me around in a circle as if we were dancers. We hugged, kissed, laughed, and cried. He, too, had experienced a miracle.

Dad, dressed in bluish overalls with the sleeves rolled up, appeared worn out, laboring all day and night for the war effort, making boots for the Soviet military. He asked me why I was in Kiev, what the journey was like, and how the family was. For the next thirty minutes or so, I breathlessly filled him in on all the details.

Father then took me to his boss's office, where Dad explained to him who I was and how my family came to be separated. My father asked his boss if he could go back with me to the collective so that he could be with his wife and children. Father also pointed out to his boss that he didn't want his daughter to make the return trip to camp alone. His boss said that would not be possible. The army needed him right now, plus there would be all sorts of discharge papers that would require a few weeks' time to complete. So after eating a decent meal, I slept that night in my father's room with the understanding that I would return to Mother and Bernie the next morning.

After a thankfully uneventful train ride back to the collective, I told Mother about all that had happened on my adventures to and from and in Kiev. She was so proud of me. I was proud that I had accomplished what I had intended to do. Everyone wanted to hear the details of my journey to Kiev, and I loved sharing all the anecdotes with them.

About a month later, my father was released from his duties at the leather factory in Kiev and rejoined the family. We stayed at the collective farm for approximately six months.

As the Second World War was nearing its end in 1945, the Soviets passed a law that said all Polish citizens may return to their homes, but we didn't have a town to go back to since Trochenbrod was burned to the ground. We returned by train to neighboring Kivretz and met up with other Jews who had survived the Trochenbrod massacre and subsequent slayings. Out of a town of five thousand, there were only thirty-three survivors.

At the war's end, a Jewish organization arranged for us to be taken by train across the borders of Poland, Czechoslovakia, and Germany to a displaced persons (DP) camp. We then ended up in Linz, Austria, with other Holocaust survivors. Hundreds of refugees from all over the world arrived at this camp.

Here are my parents walking along a wooded path in 1945.

En route we saw from our train windows some of the devastation that the war had brought. When the train stopped at a town, we walked through the rubble generated by the relentless bombings. I broke my toe during one of these treks. Later, I would have toe surgery in the United States to fix it.

We were housed in barracks, and the camp had a soup kitchen. At this point, our bodies had adjusted to eating regularly, so we no longer got sick from eating as we did before. We were slowly getting our strength back. We were now free; no one wanted to kill us. We anxiously waited to settle somewhere— Cuba, South America, or the United States. Israel, still occupied by the British, would not become an independent nation until

1948, so we couldn't go there. No country seemed in a hurry to welcome Jewish immigrants as it took many months for us to leave this camp.

At the DP camp, we learned the gruesome details of the Holocaust. The full horror of the concentration camps was revealed and made us shudder, invoking anger and disbelief. We could not fathom the scale—six million Jews senselessly murdered—or the improbability that so many were ignorant of Hitler's monstrous plans. I kept asking myself—and still do: *Why was the world so silent? How could the world not know*

Dad and a friend at DP camp in 1945, wearing Soviet partisan uniforms.

I loved my parents, particularly my father, as this 1945 DP camp photograph illustrates.

what was happening? Each day at camp another survivor appeared to describe his or her ordeal.

I remember a story involving a brother who had married his sister. Unbelievably, they were not aware that they were siblings because they had survived in different camps. They somehow ended up in the same DP camp. The couple found out they were sister and brother from a registry in a Jewish newspaper much later, but before they had any children. The marriage was subsequently dissolved. There was also a woman who didn't realize that she had married her uncle. They stayed married and had a child, a daughter, who lived in Florida.

There are Christians walking along the streets of Europe who don't know that they are Jewish. Many Jewish parents gave their babies to Christian families, and these parents didn't return to claim them. These individuals don't know that they are Holocaust survivors. If parents gave away a baby who was six months old and they were later killed, the whole family was wiped out, and there was no one else around to claim the baby, that was to be expected.

Some survivors would eat anything to survive—worms and much worse. People will eat just about anything when hungry. I surely can testify to this fact. Large, strong men died like flies. They died from not getting enough food and nourishment. They were used to eating a lot. A tiny person, a thin person like me would have a better chance of not starving to death.

Many Jews committed suicide rather than risk being captured, while others killed themselves to escape hunger pains or depression. No member of our group committed suicide, but we were ready as a group to do so.

There were countless tragedies: a husband was killed, a wife was left widowed; a father was killed, a child was left alone, etc. To this day, a Jewish bulletin includes a lost-and-found column with people looking for loved ones, even after so many years.

On the positive side, however, I met lots of other children at camp. There was a social hall where we danced and played games. I even had a boyfriend. We found ways to pass the time.

Yet we were anxious to leave the camp. It was crowded—ten families to each barrack. After several months in camp, Father decided to send a telegram to relatives in Cleveland. My mother had two sisters and a brother and lots of nephews and nieces in that city. However, he didn't remember any addresses. He was not schooled in English, so he wrote down whatever he could recall. He remembered the name Harry Abrams, who was married to my mother's sister, Rose, so he spelled the words phonetically.

Luckily, Western Union received the telegram in Cleveland and made an effort to locate Harry Abrams, who, fortunately, retrieved the telegram. The Abrams were elated that we were alive. The whole family had a meeting and sent us affidavits, promising the U.S. government that they would take care of us. They would have to guarantee, however, that we would not be a burden to the United States government.

We came to America on September 1, 1946, on the ship *Marine Perch*. The boat ride across the Atlantic was miserable and took about nine or ten days. On the first night the crew gave us a big meal, which we devoured, but Mother and I got so sick that we never ate again on the ship. I vomited throughout much of the trip and was so sick that I wanted to jump off the ship. Bernie and Dad, on the other hand, felt fine. We slept on pieces of canvas rather than beds.

I'll never forget the entrance to New York City. At first there was silence among the passengers, but when the Statue of Liberty appeared, people stood and cheered. More than a few cried. I thought to myself, *Can it be true? Am I really in America?*

After the ship docked and we walked onto the pier, I felt I had arrived in an exotic new world. In a few minutes I saw automobiles and tall buildings. I even saw a woman driving a car, which was unthinkable where I came from. I said to myself at that moment that I would have a car someday when I was old enough. That's what I would do, and that's what I eventually did.

We went through Ellis Island. All refugees had to go through Ellis Island to fill out documents and get physical exams. Our names were only slightly changed; Potazh became Potash.

During the checkup doctors discovered a spot on my mother's lung from a bout of tuberculosis she survived when she was a child. "Well, your mother has to go back to Germany," they said. "But the three of you can stay in America."

And we said, "If she goes back, we go back. If she stays, we stay." We didn't budge.

Well, we didn't know what would happen. The authorities gave us a room at Ellis Island while my parents got in touch with our relatives in Cleveland. My parents explained to the Abrams that we couldn't leave Ellis Island because of our mother's health history. Our Cleveland family decided to drive to New York to see what could be done. One relation, a cousin, was a physician.

We stayed for two weeks at Ellis Island, sleeping in bunk beds at night. The officials gave us fifty cents a day and provided a little snack bar where you could buy things. They fed us in a big hall. The refugees and immigrants came from all over the world, especially Europe, which had been devastated by the recent war.

Finally, the Abrams arrived at Ellis Island and persuaded the authorities to let my mother officially enter the country along with the rest of the Potashes. The Abrams promised that they would take my mother for treatment in Denver, so we all got into the car and headed toward Cleveland. I got sick to my stomach as I suffered from car sickness and threw up much of the time on my trip to my new hometown.

A whole new life was about to unfold for a sixteen-year-old girl and her immigrant family.

CHAPTER FOUR

MY TESTIMONY

✳ I didn't want to forget. I refused to forget. Before falling asleep each night in the forest and later in Cleveland, I would try to remember each person's name and house from Trochenbrod. I did this for years and years, and then little by little the names started to fade. I still know a lot of them, but I have forgotten many. In retrospect, I made the big mistake of not writing down the names of my townspeople when their faces were still fresh in my memory.

I am not alone in trying to preserve the images. I spoke recently with Enia, my eighty-eight-year-old cousin and a fellow Trochenbroder. She said, "I still remember where every house was. I still remember everybody. I still remember everyone's name. Every night I think about them."

My recollections have been enhanced, however. After second- and third-generation Trochenbroders visited the area several times, including most recently for a film documentary, I now have a list of all the people who were killed in our town. I also have a map. Now I will be able to place houses with the people who lived in them—all the people who were killed and those who survived.

Only thirty-three people survived the massacres. Some survived by following the Soviets when they left; others went to Siberia or China. Shanghai had a large Jewish refugee community. A few others escaped death by hiding in Christian families' houses. Some stayed alive by roaming through villages, and a tiny few, like us, hid in the forest.

One person survived in an interesting way. This young lady possessed natural blonde hair and blue eyes, which was unusual for a Jew. She claimed to be a Polish Christian and held signed papers documenting that she was Polish. She spoke Polish perfectly. You could never tell from her looks and speech that she was Jewish. She had to be on her guard and hide her Jewish background all the time, but she survived because of her looks. She worked for some sort of Polish dignitary, who knew she was really Jewish, but he didn't betray her by turning her in. She was lucky that he helped her. They weren't a couple as some might have thought; she was a single woman. She is still alive and lives in Ukraine as a Polish citizen.

There were several babies who avoided death, babies that Jewish families gave to Christian families so their children would not be killed. The Jews had known these families before the Holocaust and they were friends. "Look, we are young people who might be killed. Take our babies."

I knew of one couple who asked a Christian family to take their baby in case they were killed. "If we stay alive, then we'll come and get the baby. If not, the baby will be yours," they told the Christians. They made a deal. They gave them some money. Sadly, this beautiful young couple was killed, and this Christian family kept the baby.

We knew that this Jewish couple had given their baby girl to the Christian couple. After the war ended, my father went to claim the child for an uncle. The father's brother escaped to Israel after the war, and the uncle wanted that child, his brother's child.

So my father paid a visit to the Christians. He knew who they were, where they lived, where the child lived. My father told them, "You know there were only a very few survivors. The baby's parents were killed. But there's an uncle in Israel who would love to have the child. He wishes to adopt the little girl." But the Christians didn't want to give up the child because they had become extremely attached to her. The girl was about three years old by then.

Certain Jewish organizations were finding orphans here and there in Christian orphanages and other places, and these children would be shipped to Israel. They would pay money to the Christian people who took care of the babies as a sign of gratitude. My father said, "If you give us the child, we'll ship it to Israel, and you will get some money." I don't know how much they would have been paid. So my father went and asked for the baby.

In this instance, this couple said no. But the uncle was determined, by hook or by crook, to get the child, his brother's child, the only survivor from the entire family. It really is difficult sometimes for me to talk about it. After the couple's refusal to give up the little girl, a group of men decided that something had to be done to get this child to the uncle. The only solution was to kidnap her.

Understandably, it was heartbreaking for the Christian family, who had protected and raised the girl, to hand over the child to someone else. On the other hand, this child was a Holocaust survivor whose family was murdered. Why should the family lose this girl to a Christian upbringing when she's Jewish? Strong arguments existed on both sides.

The uncle's family and friends were very sympathetic toward the Christian family. However, they chose to kidnap the little girl and leave money in an envelope, so they did and took the child to Israel.

After they got the child, the uncle got in touch with the Christian family. He told them that if they wished, he would bring her over to visit. They could also keep in touch, send pictures, etc. The girl did correspond with her Christian family. They remained very close, and she returned for visits several times. My parents had been to Israel and had seen the child. I have visited Israel and seen her myself. She is now a married woman with three children. She has quite a story of her own!

In retrospect, a new generation of Jews was saved because these Christian families and others bravely and lovingly took care of the Jewish children while their parents fled.

The young mother who suffocated her toddler daughter while we hid behind the wall died recently at 101 years old. Maybe God punished her forever for this act. She lost her children, and her husband died of cancer. She had to live the rest of her life with these personal tragedies. Perhaps this was part of her atonement. She had a niece in Israel, her husband's brother's daughter. The niece and I are very close. Her son gave the eulogy at his great aunt's funeral and talked about these tragic events of the Holocaust and what she had accomplished. She built a synagogue, a hospital, and a nursery school in memory of her children. She and her husband were exceptionally philanthropic and generously donated much money for many causes. They had made a lot of money in America and then immigrated to Israel.

I got a phone call from her niece in Israel. She asked me, "When did Mendel's children die? When did they get killed?" I told her that it was at the Yom Kippur killing. She said there was a rumor that her aunt had suffocated a child, and she called me to verify it. The niece didn't say "the little girl." I told her that there was a mother who suffocated her little child, and I left it at that. The niece told me that she had heard that her aunt had also suffocated her other children, the two sons. I told her that it was not true, that the boys were killed during the Yom Kippur massacre.

I now I have a problem. My father, mother, and brothers were witnesses, but they are all dead. I'm the only witness left. The Trochenbrod community and all the descendants know the story. I'm in a desperate situation. I can't stop talking about this event because it is all documented. She's very old and not in good health. Do I tell her the truth? That would be the right thing to do. I live with such guilt and mixed emotions. I usually stay with her when I visit Israel. I can't tell her over the phone, but if I were in Israel visiting, I would. She would be ashamed to find out the truth. I receive many responses from people who don't understand how a mother could do such a terrible thing.

✳ ✳ ✳

My mother had two sisters and a brother, and we stayed with her sister Rose Abrams and her husband Harry in Cleveland Heights. They celebrated our arrival from Europe with an open house for the entire extended family—more than a hundred people, including many cousins. From that group, only two of us are still alive today. Harry Abrams, who was financially well off, made a lot of money through real estate.

We stayed in the Abrams' house for about two weeks. Then they found a little apartment for us, near where streetcars used to park, on East 123rd and Superior Avenue in Cleveland in a building that they owned. We lived on the third floor in three tiny rooms: kitchen, living room, and Mom and Dad's bedroom. My brother slept in the dining room, while the small sofa in the living room was my bed.

These modest accommodations didn't bother us. We didn't care; we were happy. No one wanted to kill us, and we had food. Nor were we afraid of hard work. We understood and appreciated the fact that in this country we all shared the same opportunities as everyone else.

My father was an orthodox man who refused to work on the Sabbath. A cousin of ours told him, "Eli, if you don't, you will never be able to make a living." He told her that "No one will have to support me; I will find a way." He never worked a Saturday in his life and he did all right. My father held fast to his beliefs and was a man of principle; he did things his way.

The Abrams were expected, as part of the agreement with the government, to take care of us. They knew people who owned a luggage factory in downtown Cleveland, so, luckily for us, Dad soon found employment. Father would take the nearby streetcar to work.

A long time later, my father decided to start his own business, making luggage, upholstery, cornices, and a variety of leather items, so he opened a shop on East 123rd Street. Father's strong work ethic enabled the family to move from our small apartment to a house on Lakeview Road. In the beginning it was tough, but Dad made a modest living. However, the shop didn't succeed and eventually had to be closed.

Father then became a carpenter. Somebody who knew somebody gave him a job. He worked eight hours on the job in the sun and the heat and the cold, mostly helping to construct new homes and buildings. As if this job weren't time-consuming and difficult enough, he would come home, quickly eat some supper, and hurry out to do remodeling to make extra money, building kitchen cabinets and completing a wide range of carpentry projects. People always had something to be fixed, and he became known for the quality of his craftsmanship, yet he continued to struggle financially.

Then one day, he decided to make a two-family house out of our home on Lakeview, so that he could rent out the back while we lived in the front. He got a little income from that. Soon after he went to one of my aunts and borrowed $2,000. He had saved $1,000 and now had enough for a down payment. He bought his first house with that money.

Dad continued working and collecting rent to pay the mortgage. Eventually, he bought three houses: a two-family, a four-family, and a six-family. Like my Uncle Harry, Father found that good money could be made in the real estate business. Dad was not a rich man, but he made a very nice living after many rough years of trying to make ends meet.

While we continued to adjust to our new home, we discovered some terrible yet not totally unexpected news. Some refugees told us that my older brother had died. One of these refugees had served in the same Soviet partisan unit as Shiman on the war front. He told us that Shiman was killed during the fighting. I never learned the exact circumstances of my brother's death. Maybe my parents were given more details that were never shared with Bernie and me.

To this day, I have this fantasy that whenever I'm in a crowd, going to a theater or someplace, I would bump into him. Sometimes I'm in bed, and I have an image that he is going to walk through my door at night and surprise me. It's ridiculous. I'm grown up; I should not entertain such childlike imaginings. Why should I dream about the possibility when I know it's not realistic? There were witnesses when Shiman died. I often thought that maybe I'd run into him someday, but, I would ask myself, would I even recognize him?

I was in the elevator the other day and thought what if the elevator door opened and Shiman was standing there? Of all the people who were killed, I think mostly of him. For years and years, before we learned he had died, I thought that I would meet up with him.

Despite my brother's death, we were lucky that we were a unit: a mother, a father, and two kids. Bernie and I were the only children from Trochenbrod who had a set of parents still alive. The boys who survived the Holocaust wanted to marry only those refugee girls who had parents. It meant that they were protected—that they hadn't been raped.

I remember how happy I was to come to America—so much food and so many shops. Yet life was difficult for me because I had no friends. I did, however, make some friends at John Hay High School. In order to attend public school, refugees to the Cleveland area had to learn English at John Hay in a six-month course taught by Mrs. Glick. Other courses to help immigrants assimilate into society were also offered. Immigrant teenagers from all over the world, particularly Europe, were enrolled. So between my classes at John Hay and speaking and listening to neighbors and friends in the Jewish–American community, I was able to improve my English enough to enter a regular school.

Because I didn't speak English well enough, I couldn't go directly to high school and had to first attend Roosevelt Junior High School, where, embarrassingly, I was the oldest student in the building. Some kids made fun of me because I was an outsider, a refugee, a displaced person. We immigrants didn't

Here I am (second from right) with a group of immigrants at Cleveland's John Hay High School in 1946, studying to improve our English.

have the loafers or the pleated skirts or lipstick or whatever was fashionable, so some kids bullied us.

I was made fun of a little bit at Cleveland Heights High School. I was picked on because I was a greenhorn, a newly arrived immigrant. There were snobs, and I found it difficult to make friends with students who were not refugees like me. Few people wanted to talk with me. I had to eat alone in the cafeteria because I didn't have the kinds of clothes other girls wore, was not well groomed, and spoke broken English. I would often return home from school and cry. In fact, I often escaped my loneliness and sadness by going to the movie theater, where I sat alone in the balcony so that no one could see me cry.

But my sorrow was temporary. Not being accepted by my peers gave me courage. I got angry. I thought to myself, *Someday, you wait and see. I'll get even with you guys, you who laugh at me.* I knew someday that I would surprise my detractors and become successful because I worked very, very hard to do well in school and to graduate as soon as possible. Ambition and determination had always driven me to establish goals and to follow my dreams.

On the other hand, it was a little easier for Bernie to adjust, to make friends. Maybe it was easier because he was a boy or two years older or because he had a carefree spirit. I don't know.

My brother and I worked every day after school till nine o'clock. We split our meager earnings—sixty cents an hour— with our parents to help pay the bills. I worked at a bakery, and Bernie worked for a catering service. My brother and I spent our incomes on school passes, personal grooming items, and a few clothes.

We were overwhelmed by the quality of life here compared to our experiences prior to coming to America. I thought one grocery store could feed the entire world! Not only did we appreciate the easy availability of food but, more importantly, we treasured two personal freedoms that were granted to us: freedom of speech and freedom of religion. We Potashes recognized and cherished the opportunities that our new homeland provided.

As my English improved, I tried harder to fit in. I now wanted to have only American friends. In the eleventh grade I met a boy—American born, naturally—whom I didn't like that much, but who was very nice to me. I met him through his brother, who went to school with my brother. They did homework together.

One day my brother's friend was going to give me a ride to the library, but he couldn't go, so he sent his older brother instead. I was about seventeen. After that he started to call me. Little by little, we started to date. I never had the opportunity to date anyone else. He introduced me to his friends and showed me a good time. He was always around, driving me everywhere in his father's car and helping me with my homework.

After dating him for almost a year, I thought *How am I going to get out of this?* I supposed that I would have to marry him because in European tradition, when a couple dated, they eventually got married. In Europe, we did not have such a thing as dating more than one person. You didn't go from boy to boy or from girl to girl. This custom did not exist. You found a first girlfriend or boyfriend, you went together, and then you got married. I thought that's what I was supposed to do. When I try to analyze it now, I see how silly it was. I was following European rather than American tradition.

Before I got involved with this young man, one of my aunts tried to fix me up with a young doctor. I declined because I possessed no self-confidence. I didn't think I was good enough to go out with a doctor. My self-esteem was bruised from my Trochenbrod experiences and from the prejudice I encountered when I arrived in this country. In fact, I don't think I've met any Holocaust survivor who was not psychologically damaged in some way. Many have sought the help of therapists, as I have, to overcome a range of personal and emotional issues.

I was nineteen, and he was twenty-one in 1948, the year we were married. People got married young in those days, but if I had a daughter, I would be very upset with her if she had done what I did. What a mistake! In those days a lot of people graduated from high school and got married right away. But in my heart, I knew he wasn't the right man. I didn't ask my parents for their permission to marry. Had I done so, they probably would have said no. I wish my folks had interfered, had told me that marrying this man wasn't a good idea. I don't know why I went ahead and married him when I sensed I shouldn't have. I can't understand it. I got smarter much later, unfortunately.

My parents couldn't afford a wedding, so Aunt Rose organized the event. Five hundred people must have attended. Many people whom I didn't know were there. People from all over the country, including Trochenbroders—those who escaped before the Holocaust—came to "see the monkey out of the forest." Guests wanted to see the Holocaust survivors. I didn't know many of the people who came.

With my bouquet shaking nervously in my hand, I walked down the aisle in a dress I borrowed from a cousin. Everyone was crying for the little girl who survived the Holocaust. I felt as though people were attending a funeral instead of a wedding. It was just a poor man's wedding, no sit-down dinner, just punch and cake. I didn't know the difference, so it wasn't important to me that it wasn't a fancy wedding.

I'll never forget, while dancing with a cousin at my wedding, when he sarcastically asked, in reference to my husband, "Where did you pick him up?" I was startled and upset at this question, which was asked in all seriousness. My cousin's words, as rude as they seemed at the time, ultimately proved to be perceptive.

We went to New York City for our honeymoon, and this is when I began to realize that I probably should not have jumped into this marriage. We stayed at a popular honeymoon location back then—the Barbizon Plaza. It wasn't a pleasant honeymoon. We visited friends and then stayed the last few days with a friend of mine from Europe. While I remained with my European friend and some of her friends, my husband went downtown to see the shows. Why was it okay with me? I don't understand why I accepted this arrangement—on a honeymoon of all things! At the time, I didn't make much of it—I really didn't. It didn't dawn on me that he was very immature, that I was being taking advantage of, and that he didn't really care about me.

During our first year of marriage we lived with my in-laws. My husband got a job as a traveling salesman, which put him on the road five days a week. As a newlywed this wasn't much fun. My husband's younger brother also lived in the same house, making for crowded living conditions. We could not afford to pay rent; however, we paid his parents $15 a week for room and board. Fortunately, my husband's family adored me. I loved my father-in-law. My own family, on the other hand, did not care for my husband. For a short while I worked at an office, and my father-in-law kindly drove me to and from work.

We came back from our honeymoon, and three months later I was pregnant. My mother-in-law said to me, "Why did you have to get pregnant so soon?" She was right, of course, but these were not the words of support I needed. I didn't have an answer. I didn't know why. But I was hurt because I didn't want to get pregnant. My own parents were not thrilled either by the pregnancy, but at least they didn't express their concerns to me directly. They were actually hoping that a divorce would precede a baby.

I was in labor for nineteen hours, and my husband never showed up. Perhaps in those days that was not so unusual. After the birth of our son Michael, on September 18, 1949, I woke up to tell my husband the news. I was overwhelmed with love and joy when the little bundle was placed in my arms. The feeling was indescribable.

After nine days in the hospital, I came home to my parents' home to recuperate. Great excitement followed Michael's birth as he was the first grandchild, first nephew, first cousin, and the first child born to a Holocaust survivor in Cleveland. After three weeks the baby and I returned to my in-laws' house, where Michael found a house full of people anxious to spoil him.

With my husband on the road and me stuck in the house, I became restless. I felt tied down. That is when I decided to join a synagogue and its choir. It was one of the best decisions I have ever made for several important reasons.

As traditional as I was in Trochenbrod, after the war I lost my faith. I was angry at God for all the suffering my family and other Jewish families experienced during the Holocaust. How could God allow such a nightmare to happen to innocent people? However, little by little, my faith returned. My mother and father were also active in the synagogue, but Bernie wasn't. With the synagogue came traditions. Once again, as I did in Trochenbrod, I celebrated the Jewish traditions and holidays. I met other couples with whom I became lifelong friends. I organized a "Cousins Club." I became involved in arranging many parties and gatherings that have provided so many special memories.

In 1952, my in-laws decided to buy a two-family house in Cleveland Heights. They moved in on the first floor, and we rented the upstairs floor at a special rate—$37 a month. My husband got a new job while I remained a busy housewife, throwing parties, socializing, and becoming an active member of the local chapter of B'nai B'rith, a worldwide Jewish community service organization. This group, which met in the evenings, gave me the chance to satisfy my need to accomplish something, mostly raising funds for women's needs. I would eventually become an officer.

Another son, Sheldon, was born on January 18, 1954. After I came home from the hospital, my husband informed me that he had quit his job and found a new one. I was furious because that was about the fourth job that he either quit or was fired from. This new job took him on the road again, which he didn't mind at all. Now I had two children and no husband around to help. As a traveling salesman, if there were emergencies, he would not be there. In the meantime, I became very ill from bleeding ulcers and blood transfusions and had to be hospitalized. Thank God, my brother-in-law, who—unlike his brother—had both feet on the ground, was around to assist. He loved my babies. He was a godsend in so many ways.

The person who rescued me the most during these hectic times was my cleaning lady, Althea. An absolute angel, she was always there when I needed her. I really couldn't afford to pay her well, but she just wanted to help. She was family—we loved her and she loved us. When I was in the hospital, Althea took care of the kids.

A problem developed when my husband returned after working two weeks on the road. The boys did not welcome their father with open arms. They resented his being away from home so much and in not taking any interest in their lives. He didn't like their attitude. I suggested that he find work in town to be closer to the family, but he refused. Tension increased between us. I just stopped depending on him.

Around this time, I started taking courses and eventually became a nursery school teacher. I found the nursery school job through a friend of mine. I attended classes and earned a two-year degree, becoming a member of the nursery school association. I couldn't wait to teach and also make a little money. But I got pregnant again, which stopped my plans. My husband had persuaded me into trying one more time to have a girl. Well, we welcomed another son, Allan, on December 18, 1956.

I can't say that I had a good marriage. My husband, a talented musician who could play many instruments by ear, was a free spirit, the life of the party, and extremely bright and well read, but he was not a family man. He wasn't a responsible husband and father. We probably married too young. He was not as traditional as I wanted him to be. He also did not support me in my efforts to maintain Jewish traditions and to attend synagogue.

He was not a Holocaust survivor but an American. Like me, he came from a traditional home, but, like I've said, he was a free spirit. I guess I should have married someone more like my father. My husband and I were so different from each other. I was more ambitious and worked harder. Family and synagogue were important to me. I had to push my kids to go to Hebrew school and encourage them in their studies. He was not orthodox and neither was I, but I was a conservative Jew. My husband didn't care if we went to synagogue or if the kids went to Hebrew school.

Believe me, no child wants to go to Hebrew school. No kid wants to get on a bus after a long day at public school and go to Hebrew school, so I had to encourage them myself. I wanted them to learn about their culture and religion and forced them to go. They did well, especially Shelley.

Lenny, my husband's brother, was the exact opposite of my husband. He was like my father. He was there for my children, and my children loved him. He was a father figure for my sons since their own father frequently neglected his responsibility in raising them. When Uncle Lenny battled cancer for a couple of years, my boys were there day and night for him, nursing him until the day he died. In gratitude for their affection, Lenny made tapes about my children, about how much he loved and appreciated them for being there for him during his illness. And he made a tape about me, too.

My husband and I were married for twenty-eight years and divorced in 1976. I didn't date for many years after the split because my kids were younger and because I usually worked and was always involved in some activity. Divorce was not as common then. My father knew that I married the wrong person, but as long as my spouse was Jewish, he was happy. His only request to his children was that they marry into the faith. None of his children married out of the faith, but his grandsons married Christian girls. I'm not sure how my father would have reacted to that. Not too well, I suppose. As long as my husband was Jewish and a decent enough fellow, Father didn't interfere, even though he knew I married the wrong man. My dad never ridiculed me or criticized me for marrying this man. He kept his disapproval to himself. He was cordial to my husband, and they got along well.

On the other hand, my mother disliked my husband and the marriage. Perhaps to get back at her for not liking my husband, I think I stayed longer in the marriage than I would have otherwise. She would disparage my husband, not to his face, but to me. My husband knew that my parents wanted something better for me. Being old-fashioned in those days, you accepted the fact that when you got married, you married for life. But now, as I look back on my situation, I would not give the same advice. If I had a child who was in a marriage as broken as mine, then I would advise my child to get out of it. If you're not happy in a marriage, then you shouldn't continue in it.

My three sons—Michael, Allan, and Sheldon (left to right)—and I were at Allan's 1981 wedding.

I've learned from personal experience that one must not be ashamed or embarrassed if a marriage doesn't work out. I didn't complain to my parents because I was embarrassed. I saw the failure that was my marriage when I compared it to other marriages around me. I don't regret everything about my marriage because it did produce three magnificent sons. But if I could turn the clock back, I can't say that I would do it in the same way with what I know now.

Another factor that contributed to my unhappy marriage was that when I came to America, almost all refugees married other refugees. There were refugee clubs in every major city. Here the immigrants met and socialized and ended up marrying each other. Marrying a fellow immigrant made adjusting to American culture easier because both partners would be especially empathetic to the other's background and challenges. It was rare for a refugee to marry an American as I did. There were rarely divorces among these refugee partnerships. My husband asked questions about my past, but never truly understood my Holocaust experiences.

More damaging to our marriage was how my husband treated our oldest son, Michael. He abused him, physically and verbally, all the way through high school. I still live with the guilt that I didn't leave my husband right then and there. I can't understand where my mind was. Why wasn't I brave enough to act? Hadn't I already seen this behavior with my own father when he beat up my brother Shiman? Instead of taking action, I kept quiet and shut the windows so nobody would hear the screams. Like my father, interestingly, my husband never laid a hand on the other kids.

I have apologized to Michael, but I will carry the guilt to my grave. My husband neither drank nor did drugs. He didn't display a bad temper with me and treated me pretty well. But he didn't have any confidence in himself; maybe that is what triggered his anger. He was the black sheep of his family. Everybody else seemed more successful in their jobs, while he jumped from one job to another. Perhaps my husband took out these insecurities on his son.

I can't understand why I wasn't strong enough then to stand up on behalf of my child or on behalf of myself. What made me just watch and cry and not try to protect my child? But I couldn't stop it. Michael said to me years later, "Mom, those were different times then. People were embarrassed. People didn't talk about it. Now, if something like this happens, mothers and families know what to do." So Michael tried to comfort me. "It's not your fault, Mom. Stop beating yourself," Michael would tell me. He was a wonderful son. But I will never forgive myself. It is the worst thing that I lived with until Allan committed suicide. Now, it's the second worst thing.

As a child in Lutsk I saw big-shot people—businessmen—in the city, and I wanted to be sophisticated like them. As I grew older, I no longer wanted to be a dancer as I had imagined as a young girl while visiting Lutsk with my father. Instead, I wanted to pursue a business career. I also regretted not continuing my education, but I would find an outlet for my ambitious streak through a number of occupations.

I taught nursery school for ten years at Carroll Nursery on Green Road, in a rented space in a synagogue. I was paid $12.50 for an afternoon's work. As a perk, my three kids were enrolled for free. My husband was earning enough for me to work part-time. Their interest in sports developed when I began to teach nursery school. I was hired by a swim club to run the nursery school, where the parents came and dropped off their children. So I ran the nursery school and took advantage of the opportunity for my sons to join the swim club for free. My boys also attended a number of summer camps that were offered through the school.

I became a businesswoman in my thirties through a cousin of mine, who owned a lingerie business. She wanted to have more free time for herself and asked me if I would buy into the business and become a partner. At that time, the job didn't pay much. My father was thrilled about the idea and lent me $10,000 even though he had reservations about me working. I paid him back in a couple of years.

We sold fancy designer lingerie, and business picked up

enough that we opened two more stores on Cleveland's east side. The original was on Van Aken Boulevard, another was at Eton on Chagrin Boulevard, and one was in Chagrin Falls. I was running back and forth, managing three stores. We did reasonably well financially, and I made enough money to support myself and the boys after my husband and I divorced.

At this time, my mother was ill with leukemia, so I didn't work for an entire summer to take care of her. Mother was dying, so I wanted to spend the summer with her. I partnered with my cousin for ten years before she became sick with lung cancer. Because she knew she was dying, we agreed to sell the business.

After my mother died, I got a call from a gentleman, who knew I was a businesswoman. He asked me if I wanted to work for him. That's when I joined a textile company. I did very well with them. They're still in business. I was top dog, making more money than any other sales representative. There was a lot of traveling. My sons were out of the home—either in college (my youngest) or married—so leaving town wasn't a problem. But with the job came a lot of sexual harassment.

Because I was a woman, the men at the office couldn't accept my success and verbally harassed me. They called me names; they would call me "princess" or "bitch." They were jealous because I was a woman and achieved more than they did. There was an employee who would pinch my behind all the time. Despite being harassed, I didn't pay attention to this sorry individual.

I remember one occasion when I brought textile samples from a sales trip and placed them in the warehouse for the manager to examine. After examining these samples, the manager lost interest in the product and demanded that I put the samples where they belong, which was not what I was being paid to do.

I firmly advised him that he "put the samples back where they belong. I don't have time for that. My time is valuable. My time is to make sales." He turned around and called me a bitch.

After months of this kind of treatment, finally, out of desperation, I went to my boss and complained. He said, "Oh, don't pay attention. They're just jealous." I said, "No, you have to talk to them. Please get them to stop it." My boss said that he "didn't want to start a commotion." He was an old-fashioned businessman.

I couldn't take it anymore, so I sought out a legal agency and filed a complaint. They sent my boss a report. They told him that if this were to happen again, he would be sued. My boss called me in when he got the letter and asked me, "Why did you do that?" I said, "It's because I complained to you many times and you didn't say anything on my behalf. You never stopped it. I couldn't take it anymore. I warned you." He said, "Okay, I'll see what I can do." I said, "Why did you have to wait for the letter? Why couldn't you have done something for me before?" He said that he "didn't want to start anything."

There was a meeting, and he said a couple of words to the men that didn't mean very much. He said that we have to "get along with another," we have to "respect each other," blah, blah, blah. The job was very important to me. It was my livelihood. Where would I go if I left the company? I was afraid to quit.

I lasted at the company for twenty-one years—until I couldn't take it anymore. In the beginning, it wasn't bad, and I started to make more money when I began to learn the business. As I became more and more successful, the better it was for me financially, but the harder it was for me personally because of the harassment.

I worked in the office more than I was on the road, but we presented our products at exhibits in Columbus and other cities. I'd exhibit the merchandise, and hotel owners, managers, and buyers would view the products. We did this a few times a year, and that's when I traveled away from the Cleveland office. If a hotel or nursing home wanted to decorate their rooms, I would drive, if it were within a four-hour drive, to these places and take samples with me. But if it were farther, I would ship the samples by UPS and fly and work with the buyer or decorator or whomever and fly back.

There was no pension; I retired from this company without a penny. My boss promised all sorts of deals. I nearly had to beg for a commission. He said that we would have a 401K. He kept promising and promising, but he never acted on that, so when I retired, I had nothing. After twenty-one years, I had no pension, no health care, or anything. I was on my own.

Later in life, following the divorce, I developed a relationship with someone who reminded me of my father. The man was an American, not a Holocaust survivor. He was very old-fashioned and, like my father, hard-working and conscientious. When I met him he had been separated from his wife for many years; he lived on his own in an apartment while his wife and three children lived elsewhere with their mother. I met his children, but not as their father's girlfriend. No one knew that he and I were having a relationship. My own children did not know either because they were already out of the house at that time.

I think that the reason he didn't get divorced was because of money. I didn't know exactly. It had something to do with what he had to pay or give his wife if they were divorced. I never asked him to explain why he wouldn't get a divorce. I really didn't care because all that mattered was that I was madly in love with him. I would have lived anywhere with him. He felt the same for me. We never seriously discussed marriage, but we had a few conversations about what it would be like if we were married. My friend and I went out to dinner and to the movies occasionally, but mostly it was the companionship that we enjoyed.

The relationship lasted fourteen years. Those were the best years of my life—after he died, I couldn't even look at another man. I wasn't interested in romance anymore. He was the only man that I truly ever loved.

My life has had its share of tragic events, but none was more painful than the one in October 2010, when Allan, my youngest son, committed suicide. Shortly after his passing, I lived up to my obligations at the Maltz Museum of Jewish Heritage in Beachwood and my other volunteer work. I went through with those commitments even though it was very difficult for me. Avrom Bendavid-Val, author of *The Heavens Are Empty: Discovering the Lost Town of Trochenbrod*, was coming to town from Washington, D.C., to give two presentations, one at Saint Ignatius High School and the other at the Maltz Museum, and he wanted me to join him since I contributed so much to his book. We were also interviewed on a local Cleveland radio show, "Around Noon," on the NPR affiliate, WCPN.

Allan, named after an uncle, was in commercial real estate. He would buy a house, fix it up, and then rent it out or sell it. Allan and his wife adopted a son, Nikolai, from Russia. I just came back from Atlanta, where Allan lived. The occasion was Grandparents Day, and the visit was difficult. I seemed to do all right when I visited my grandson's school. I was able to talk to Nikolai's teachers, who gave me excellent reports on his progress. He is doing very well. I also enjoyed watching his basketball team's practice. He's a very good basketball player. We went out to eat, and that was good for me as well. Being with Nikolai lifted my spirits and, I hope, his. I stayed with my daughter-in-law, my son's ex-wife. We are still on very good terms.

But other than these moments with my grandson, this was the first time I'd been to Atlanta since my son killed himself, and it was horrible. I just couldn't stop crying day and night, of course, when no one saw me. I couldn't wait to leave Atlanta and go home. It was very hard, and still is, accepting the fact that I won't see Allan again.

There is so much missing in my life now that Allan is gone. I've gotten some measure of comfort from a book titled *The Next Place*, written by Warren Hanson. It was given to me after the funeral. It's so beautiful—it's an amazing book. I have bought copies for people I know who could use it.

When I listen to Allan's final voice mail to me, I feel in a strange sense that he is living inside that answering machine. Allan had already killed himself when I came home to hear these words: "Mom, I love you very much. You are a saint. I'm very sorry about the way I'm ending my life. I know that it's going to hurt you so much. I just can't go on any longer with my life. I'm sorry that I'm leaving Nikolai and Shelley. I love you, Mom. Goodbye, and live in peace."

Allan's son doesn't talk about his father very much. I sent Nikolai a big box of mementos of his father. Allan won lots of awards for his many athletic accomplishments in high school. In 1975, *Seventeen* magazine came to Cleveland Heights and did a piece on what seniors in 1975 looked like—how they lived, what they wore, etc. His photograph was in that issue. I sent this magazine to Nikolai, as well as other personal items I have from Allan.

Nikolai had his bar mitzvah in June 2011, which was both a happy and sad celebration. I had mixed emotions. I wished Allan could have been there, knowing how much he loved his son. However, I kept my composure and did not cry.

My grandson is in the eighth grade and enjoys playing chess. He used to play a lot of chess with his father, and would beat him all the time. He's doing pretty well. He gets As and Bs and attends a private school, which pleases me. The school has solid standards and expectations for their students. Students can't have long hair, and there is a dress code—I love it. It reminds me so much of Saint Ignatius.

It's tough for Nikolai. At first, he was abandoned by his Russian parents and lived in an orphanage. But at eight months, he was adopted by two wonderful parents. Nothing else on earth mattered more to Allan than this child. I can't adequately describe their relationship. Nikolai always seemed to be saying, "My Daddy, my Daddy." When Nikolai's parents got divorced, Nikolai was "abandoned" again. The most tragic abandonment, of course, was the death of his father. I wonder what goes on in his little mind. How can he handle all of this pain? My heart goes out to him. I wonder how he'll do in high school. I don't know if I'll be around to see it. He must keep so much inside.

Nikolai has a loving family and friends, but I wonder how he will turn out. At the funeral, he didn't cry until they lowered the casket into the grave. His entire class came to the funeral, thank God.

When he was alive, Allan called me every single day. He'd ask, "What did you do today? Where did you speak today?" I read him letters I received. Oh my God, he was so supportive. He was so proud of me. He was being treated for depression, but he did not receive enough therapy. Allan stopped seeking treatment at the time of his suicide.

I don't think that I could continue with my life after my son's death if it weren't for the audiences, if it weren't for the responses and thank-you letters, if it weren't for being involved in the Maltz Museum. I don't think that I'd be able to carry on.

My son Allan was very supportive of my work at the museum. Shelley wasn't that interested. Michael wasn't closely involved, although he did care. Michael was the first one to come and listen to me when the museum opened. Someone asked him how I was doing and Shelley said that "she is busy speaking." "What does she speak about?" they asked Shelley. He said, "She is spreading poison." He meant that I was talking about a sensitive subject, that the speech would upset people. Shelley just didn't really care about what I was doing.

I felt that I had to complete my responsibilities, particularly those at the Maltz and at Saint Ignatius. They were too important because of Avrom's book. I don't know what gave me the strength to fulfill these duties, but my audiences were very appreciative of my not cancelling these engagements. I did avoid accepting invitations to a number of social events, including a bar mitzvah in Chicago. My anguish and heartbreak at the loss of Allan was too fresh. Having Thanksgiving at my nephew's was the first social event I attended after the tragedy. I put on a good front. I wasn't going to have anyone feel sorry for me. I tried to blend in with everyone as though nothing had happened.

It was nice to be with the family. My brother's children and grandchildren were present at the dinner. It's an amazing family. All the children are wonderful and always kind to me. My son Shelley picked me up, and we went together. They live near my home on Cleveland's east side. I was hurting inside, but I "behaved" myself. Normally, I invite family members to my place for Thanksgiving, but I didn't think it would be very pleasurable for just the two of us—Shelley and I—to eat turkey. Shelley has two sons, David and Evan; one is in California now, and the other had Thanksgiving with his mother.

Shelley is fifty-nine and his boys are in their early twenties. Shelley's two boys once heard me speak at their school in Orange. Shelley, a physical therapist and a director of physical therapy is, ironically, not in good shape. He has back and rotator cuff problems. He acts like an old man; his bones are falling apart. He's a very hard worker though; even if he's sick, he works. He is still mad at me for naming him Sheldon. He won't get over it. I've told him, "Go to court and change your name if you hate it so much. Pick another name then." I named him after my brother Shiman, the one who was killed during the war. I didn't want to name Michael, my first boy, after my brother; I was a little superstitious because Shiman had died so young. With my second one, I discussed it with my husband: "You know we probably won't have more kids." In the Jewish tradition, you name a son after a dead relative: grandfather, grandmother, whoever.

Shelley was the most responsible of my three sons. He knew that if he had to do something, he had to do it well and had to finish what he started. He was a hard worker and still is to this day. Shelley was never a problem child for me, but he was always a great worrier and remains one. He could never make a decision and was always afraid of failure. He was like a caregiver to the other boys; even though he was in the middle, he kept an eye on his brothers. Allan remained the longest with me at home.

My oldest son, Michael, was named after an uncle of my husband's. Michael, a graphic artist, had one son, Ben, who lives in Columbus. Ben received a kidney from his father, and so Ben takes a lot of medication. He's a most devoted grandson with a beautiful wife. Ben had never heard me speak formally about my experiences before a recent talk at Saint Ignatius. I was surprised that Ben was there because my son Shelley was never interested in hearing me speak. I was quite surprised, however, when Shelley appeared for Avrom's book signing at the Maltz. That was the first time that Shelley heard me tell my story. My son heard the tributes and applause that accompanied my talk, and, for the first time, he fully understood what I've been doing all these years.

Michael was fifty-six and in good health when he passed away. He died suddenly from a pancreatitis attack, surviving for only two days. They could do nothing for him. A month later, a friend of mine died of the same thing. Soon after, someone else I knew died from the same condition.

Michael left a wife with MS, and he was the caregiver. She stayed at home as long as possible, but now she lives in a nursing home with other MS residents. I call her every night.

All three sons were athletic. Michael was on the Cleveland Heights basketball team; Shelley was a champion swimmer all through high school; and Allan ran track. All were great swimmers, but Shelley was a champion swimmer.

Allan lived in Atlanta for more than twenty years. Shelley and Michael both lived here in the Cleveland area. My boys were pretty close to each other because I always told them to love each other. They remember that I always said this.

*Here I am
with my
beautiful
grandchildren
in 2009.*

Losing a child is the most difficult of all of life's tragedies, but to lose two is close to unendurable. I can't express fully the pain and sadness I've felt from these losses. I don't know what makes a person strong, what makes a person want to live, to go on. I don't know. I try not to feel sorry for myself, but I feel sorry for my son Shelley since he's an only child now.

I don't know how one survives so many tragedies. My life seems to have been one long tragedy even though I've had good years too. I'm living up to my commitments, doing what I need to do in the midst of all this crying and grief and misery, but life will never be the same. You learn to live with it.

I was able to survive another tragedy of sorts—advanced-stage lung cancer. I picked up smoking in Austria at the DP camp. A boy, another survivor, introduced me to smoking. American GIs used to give cigarettes to the men at the camp. I choked during my first puff of a cigarette. You know, smoking was fashionable then. I was sixteen. I smoked until 1985, about a pack a day for forty years. I didn't quit early enough because seven years ago I had lung cancer. The doctors blamed it on my smoking. They removed half of my left lung. Four percent of lung cancer patients survive—I survived.

I survive one thing after another. Why? Why? Is it a punishment? Am I being punished for something? That's how I feel. I really don't remember many happy years, except when my kids were older and I had a boyfriend following my divorce.

The Maltz Museum of Jewish Heritage has been around for seven years, and I was one of its first docents. I didn't tell my story very often before volunteering at the Maltz, and if I did, it was in bits and pieces. My kids' school would invite me, or I would speak at my grandchildren's schools, but for a long time, I didn't want to talk at length about Trochenbrod. I rarely disclosed the past with even my own children, and only occasionally would my relatives ask questions about Trochenbrod.

When we came here, one of my aunts complained that they didn't have enough sugar and steak during the Depression. This is partly why I refrained from discussing the Trochenbrod events. So how could I tell them my story? How would they react to stories about the suffering I went through? Comparatively, they had it pretty good.

I wanted to tell my story, but I thought that no one would understand. Also, where do I start and where do I finish? Is it really possible to tell this story? Why bother? That was my attitude. I really did not know many Holocaust survivors even though I was involved in a number of Jewish organizations. The reason I didn't know many survivors is because, regrettably, I married an American. Our social events took place among Americans. I wanted to assimilate, to achieve, to climb, to do more than other survivors did. I was asked questions occasionally about my past at these social gatherings, but I would not announce to the group, "Hey, do you want to hear my story?"

My brother Bernie was not as interested or devoted to the memory of our town or its people or the Holocaust as I was. He just didn't want to talk about Trochenbrod or the forest. He would contribute money to various Holocaust causes, but he was unwilling to discuss that horrible chapter in his life. He wanted to move on. The memories were too dark.

Yet, later in life, Bernie did something that demonstrated his devotion to his Jewish faith. As a young boy, he never had a bar mitzvah, a rite that would have admitted him as an adult member of the Jewish community, because he was hiding in the forest. So at age sixty-five, Bernie went to Israel for his bar mitzvah. In Italy, on his return to Cleveland from Israel, he suffered a fatal heart attack. His wife and one of his daughters were by his side. Despite this tragic event, all of us were comforted by Bernie's participation in this sacred ceremony. I should mention at this time that Bernie's children have been one of the major blessings in my life. They've been so good to me.

Although I would not speak publicly about the Trochenbrod massacres until much later in my life, my goal was to commit to permanent memory each face and house and place. I decided I would never forget my town. There was one survivor in Columbus and another in San Diego who were also passionate about keeping the memory of Trochenbrod alive. Don't forget that only thirty-three survived.

People would ask me questions about Trochenbrod, and I would try to answer. If I was at a meeting and the subject came up, then I would talk about it. But I never volunteered to tell my story until an opportunity presented itself.

Prior to my work at the Maltz Museum, I hadn't fully described my Holocaust experience until Steven Spielberg established, in 1994, the Survivors of the Shoah Visual Foundation and sent a crew to interview me. The video interviews are in the Holocaust Museum in Washington, D.C. Every survivor's story is kept here and available to the public. After the Shoah experience, I started to speak wherever I had an opportunity. The interview helped me to flush out all the terrible memories. When people asked me questions about being a Holocaust survivor, I became more comfortable and committed to answering those questions. Since then I'm always grateful for the chance to speak about my beloved Trochenbrod.

The Maltz Museum gave me the opportunity and setting to tell the story to a wider audience. Martha Sivertson, the Museum's director of volunteers and visitor services, encouraged me to describe the events of my childhood. Once my story got out, it spread like a brush fire. I was so busy I didn't have time for myself.

My story caught interest because most survivors talk about the concentration camps, rather than hiding and surviving in a forest. It makes my story unique. I'm not suggesting that this feature makes my story better, but this fact does underscore how broadly impacted were the victims of the Holocaust. We lost loved ones everywhere, and we all struggled and suffered terribly in our attempts to survive.

Ninety percent of the time a college or high school class will come to the Maltz after studying the Holocaust. First we go into the auditorium and I give a talk, about forty-five minutes, answering questions and so forth. Then I take them on a tour through the Holocaust exhibits. I don't have enough time to show them all the exhibits. I do this at least three times a week.

I also do speaking engagements at high schools and colleges or universities four or five times a month as well, sometimes on the same days that I'm at the Maltz. I've spoken at Ursuline College, John Carroll University, Baldwin Wallace University, Kent State University, Notre Dame College, Lake Erie College, Case-Western Reserve University, and schools outside of Ohio. I've led groups from Cleveland State University and other schools through the museum. I've spoken at the Akron City Hall, libraries, and Veterans of Foreign Wars chapters. Second World War veterans love my stories—I tell them I was a soldier, too.

I've spoken in Pennsylvania and Indiana and to groups who have come to the Maltz from out of state. I've talked about my Trochenbrod experiences to the media—radio, TV, newspapers. In October 2011 I was a guest, along with Avrom Bendavid-Val, on the "The Story," a nationally syndicated radio program from American Public Media. And many businesses, wishing to help their employees become more appreciative of diversity at the workplace, have heard my story.

Organizations invite me as a guest speaker. I hate that title because I'm not really a guest speaker. I'm not a professional. I talk. I talk "Betty Gold talk." I'm not a speaker, yet they call me a speaker. I smirk at those flyers that describe me as "Guest speaker, Betty Gold."

I've been back three times to Ukraine, where Trochenbrod was located, most recently in August 2010, to help in the production of a documentary film. I'm very fond of Jeremy Goldsheider, the filmmaker. He's a true *mensch*. I helped to clarify a number of things about Trochenbrod for Jerry. We were in Trochenbrod for about four days. Those who came to the reunion have discussed returning again. The highlight of the film documentary, one of the most wonderful moments in all my life, was finding the exact location of my house in Trochenbrod. I loved being with all the descendants—the children and the adults—and knowing that all of us there will make a difference—that also was special.

Wherever the group of Trochenbrod survivors and descendants went on these trips, we looked for lost objects from the town despite the barrenness of the surroundings. I made a craft project of sorts by putting together some of those items I brought back, including some crushed flowers. I found some little stones near my house, two pieces from the synagogue, and

Here is a 2009 photograph taken during the filming of the documen-tary on Trochenbrod, Lost Town, in Ukraine. I'm seated in the horse-drawn carriage.

My favorite photograph must be this one from 2009. Here I stand amid wildflowers at the exact location of my original Trochenbrod house.

a piece of glass from the glass factory. Shelley and Allan went with me on the second trip. My son Allan found the hardware from a door. Many of these pieces were discovered by chance by digging with our hands.

Those who invite me to speak sometimes make me feel like a celebrity. They occasionally give me chocolate, trophies, money, and flowers. I tell them not to give me these gifts. I feel uncomfortable receiving these things. I'm not a celebrity.

With the younger students the satisfaction I receive is that I offer myself as an example of what they can achieve. What I went through and what I accomplished when I came here should encourage them. I tell students today that "If I was able to overcome the challenges I've face, imagine what you can do. Unlike me you were born here with all kinds of opportunities. Anybody can accomplish anything here in this country."

In 2009, a large contingent of Holocaust survivor families from America, South America, and Israel visited Ukraine to see what was once Trochenbrod.

These images of the Trochenbrod Memorial to honor those massacred by the Nazis were taken during my 2006 visit to Ukraine.

Students in middle school, junior high, or high school come to the museum after having studied the Holocaust. The main message I try to give them is that they must stand up against prejudice, discrimination, and hatred because hatred is not something that we are born with. We don't inherit it. We learn it, so it can be unlearned.

Sadly, some of the older groups—college students and adults—really don't know much about the Holocaust. They know that the Holocaust happened, but they don't know the details. These days, unless it's a subject you've studied or you're a history major, you might not know the details. They listen to you and respond, "Oh, really? Oh my God, how could this happen?"

But how can they know? The Holocaust is impossible to understand and even more difficult to explain. I don't care how much one has read or written about the Holocaust. I don't care how many films one has seen about the tragedy or has heard about it. The Holocaust was so massively horrific that it becomes enormously difficult to describe it even adequately, let alone fully.

Over the years, I've gotten to know many survivors in Cleveland, throughout the country, and around the world. I have become friends with Elie Wiesel, Holocaust survivor and Nobel Peace Prize recipient. I didn't read Elie Wiesel's books, including his most famous, *Night,* until I met him in Washington, D.C., for a speaking engagement. Since then we have spoken in Chautauqua, New York, and at Saint Ignatius High School in Cleveland.

Besides Wiesel I've met many other people along the way: acclaimed author and dear friend, Jonathan Safran Foer, dignitaries, mayors, university professors and university presidents, and a lot of people in the educational field. I met Cleveland's mayor, Frank Jackson, because of the Jesse Owens exhibit at the

This is a photograph taken of Nobel Peace Prize recipient and friend, Elie Wiesel, and me at Saint Ignatius High School in 2007.

Maltz, which created an exhibit on the 1936 Berlin Olympics, and the renaming of a street, Jesse Owens Way, in his honor. I had lunch with Jesse Owens's daughter. So my work has introduced me to people I would otherwise not have met.

I'm the only Trochenbrod survivor living in the United States, the only person able to speak from personal experience about my town. Earlier I described my cousin Enia, who also hid in the forest for a time with my older brother and eventually landed in Lutsk after the war. She married a man from the forest, a Russian, and had a child. This child was raised Jewish and grew up to become the leader of a tiny Jewish community in Lutsk. He has a wife and two kids. I knew Enia in Trochenbrod, and later, we were reunited during my first trip back home. Actually, Avrom Bendavid-Val discovered me through Enia when he was doing research. She told him, "I have a cousin in

Cleveland. Call her." I'm so glad he did. I've been working with Avrom for quite a few years.

There are many people whom I admire, in addition, of course, to Elie Wiesel. My brother-in-law played a big part in my life. He was my role model. He was there when my husband was not. Golda Meir was someone else I admired. My dear friend Nancy Wilhelm has been a great influence. She encouraged me and pushed me to write a book. Nancy also introduced me to Saint Ignatius High School. She's truly very caring and is a blessing to me. I don't know how to show my appreciation. It's easier for Nancy to show her appreciation toward me than I for her. She expresses herself with prayers. I, on the other hand, don't talk with God. I don't express my religious beliefs. She does and I think that it's wonderful. People like her remind me of my father. It was his faith that pulled us through.

I'm a traditional Jew, not a religious Jew. I love the traditions. I enjoy the holidays, but not like before. My family is separated, living in different parts of the country. Too many don't "come to the table" these days, so now the holidays can be depressing. I have only my son in town now, and my grandsons are elsewhere. I get invitations from friends to come over for Thanksgiving and other occasions, reminding me of all the wonderful holidays I used to enjoy in my own home. I'm grateful for these invitations, but I can't accept them. I thank these kind folks, but tell them I have "other plans." I have wonderful memories of those times when we were together and celebrated the holidays, yet I miss them because I can't have them today.

Every time I think that anti-Semitism doesn't exist, something happens that reminds me it does. It does exist—right here in Cleveland, in the state, and in the country. There's one room in the Maltz Museum called the Hate Room. In the window is a figure of a Klansman with a uniform. Next to him is a little boy in the same uniform. The man is teaching his child to hate the way that he does. In the twenty-first century display, the museum lists about a dozen hate groups that exist in the United States. It's unbelievable. One map shows how many of these groups are in Ohio and where they are located throughout the United States. I accept the fact that they are permitted to demonstrate publically and to publish their racist and hateful doctrine. However, these groups leave me very discouraged, very heartsick.

As a docent at the Maltz, I actively speak against discrimination and hatred. I tell young visitors to the Maltz, in particular, that joining a gang is an example of hatred. We have to discourage students from joining gangs. We have to tell students about the dangers of being hateful. We have to tell them about discrimination.

Hate crimes and atrocities against specific groups of people begin with hatred, I tell my visitors. That's what I talk about mainly. Of course I discuss the Holocaust—I provide lots of anecdotes and examples. It still amazes me how many students are unaware or uneducated about the Holocaust. I'm surprised that so many have never heard of it. Clearly, a lot of people are still uninformed about the Holocaust. I make sure to tell my guests that the Nazis also killed gays, lesbians, and gypsies.

Can the kind of hatred and discrimination that the Nazis perpetrated happen again? Tragically, yes. Look at Rwanda, Darfur, and Cambodia. Millions were murdered in these places because of hatred and prejudice. Some of the greatest crimes against humanity have occurred in these countries.

When I watch atrocities—for example, in Haiti and other places—and cameras show the thousands of starving and malnourished infants and toddlers, I get angry at why the world doesn't educate these people in birth control. Why don't we provide them with birth control pills? There are so many babies who die before the age of five. It's heartbreaking to watch these innocent little people suffer and die out of ignorance and poverty.

I understand that there are those who believe it is against a particular religion to use birth control. That's all right. But why do they have to impose these beliefs on others? These impoverished countries wouldn't have so many babies who suffer so much and end up dying. Conflicts between religion and tradition and society upset me terribly.

I don't know why this intense level of hatred still exists. Maybe it will exist forever. People used to fight with bows and arrows, but technology has made it easier to kill more people, to destroy more places, by pushing a button. I don't know why people must continue to war against each other. Why are we in Afghanistan? The Soviets were there for nine years and failed to achieve anything. They walked out. Why are we allowing our young people to die there? Do you think that it really is solving the problem? Or are we there because of all the oil and politics? I don't like reading in the papers how many kids were killed every day. I thought people would be more civilized as we entered the twenty-first century.

I was speaking recently and a young woman, a Maltz visitor, asked me a question. I don't even remember the question. I jokingly said we would need to have lunch, dinner, or spend the week together. She said, "I would like that." Before she left, she gave me her card and said that she would love to have dinner with me. "Please call me and give me a date."

Then there are many students who approach me. "Mrs. Gold, I'm doing a project on the Holocaust. Could I interview you someday at your convenience?" They do the project, get an "A," and call me up and send me letters of thanks. I've had so many students like these over the years. I can't keep track of all of them. I feel like I'm a teacher. I get a lot of satisfaction from seeing how I've made a difference in the lives of so many.

I'm very grateful to the Maltz Museum for allowing me to do what I do, to talk about the Holocaust and especially my town and its people. That gives me the most pleasure. That has been my objective in life—to put Trochenbrod back on the map so that it will be remembered. That has always been my goal since the Second World War ended.

Over the years, my interests have helped to make my life more fulfilling. I've found comfort in these hobbies. They've provided me with the chance to invigorate my mind and soul and to allow me to escape from various hardships.

Family always came first, but traveling was second. I love traveling and have visited all seven continents. It's not like I'm "going on vacation." It's more like "I'm going to discover. I'm going to learn things." The accommodations aren't important. I like to walk into people's homes to see how the locals live and what they have to say. I like to see their wealth and their poverty, to see both the mansions and the slums. I like to go to the museums and to wander on my own. I wanted to go to India. That was my last planned trip before Allan died. I recently cancelled a trip to Israel.

I collect pottery that mean something personal to me. One was made by my second son in the second grade. Many of the pottery pieces were made by friends or family.

I just cleared out my books. I love to read, but often I don't have enough time with my frantic schedule. I keep some books in my bedroom and gave the rest to the Beachwood library. I once owned a few hundred books.

I have a subscription to the Cleveland Playhouse. I also volunteered at the Museum of Contemporary Art for eleven years, and I plan on returning as a volunteer.

I go to films sometimes if I think I'm going to like the film. Every week current films are shown here at my residence. I recently saw *Social Network* and *The King's Speech*. The latter was one of the best movies I've seen in a long time. I remember the history of the film because I was around, but I didn't know the king had a stammering problem.

Beyond these interests is my desire to be remembered as a loyal friend. I've been blessed to have so many friends, Jewish and non-Jewish—it's been a gift. I wish I could spend more time with my friends.

At times I feel as if I have a split personality—my social and private sides. In public I somehow can hide the suffering I've been through; on the other hand, when I'm alone I experience a lot of despair and regret for all that I've seen or been through in this life. *It is what it is,* I tell myself.

I loved my town and its people. Sometimes I imagine what the town would be like today. Would I still live there? Would I be living in Lutsk? Would I be in America? I'm sure I would have returned to Trochenbrod. The Nazis took me away from my town, but they can't take the town away from me.

The memories of Trochenbrod were joyfully revived recently at the reappearance of a close childhood friend, Ryszard Lubinski. Ryszard and his mother, Janina, the town's postmistress, were our dear friends and the only Christian family living in town. A local Cleveland Jewish newspaper received a

Here I am with my dear friend from childhood, Ryszard Lubinski, on the main road in Trochenbrod in 1939.

Here is a recent photograph of my dearest childhood friend, Ryszard Lubinski, and me.

letter from Ryszard, who asked if any reader had information about any survivors of his home, Trochenbrod. I was witness to another miracle! I subsequently got Ryszard's telephone number. We talked and we cried and we laughed. And a week later I flew to his Polish home to visit.

Ryszard surprised me with a gift. My grandmother had given Ryszard's mother a pair of silver saltcellars long ago, and he wanted me to have them. I can't describe their value to me—the only objects I possess from Trochenbrod.

I wish I could go back and the town still existed and the people were still there. In a sense, that will happen. Although the Jewish religion forbids cremation, I'm going to be cremated, which is a disappointment to some in my family. I want my ashes to be scattered over the mass grave at Trochenbrod.

OTHER VOICES

＊ Speaking to young people as a docent at the Maltz Museum or at schools has inspired me to continue telling my story. I'm lucky to have been a positive influence on numerous young lives for so many years. The kids have been so interested in hearing my talks and so kind in their responses that I feel a responsibility to continue delivering my testimony about the events of the Holocaust. My goal is to convince those young listeners to do something to stop all the hate in this world.

I'd like to share a few of the many hundreds of letters I've received from these beautiful children.

Dear Mrs. Gold,

I want to thank you for the amazing story you shared with us yesterday, complete with a plot, setting, main characters, and a hero—you. What made it remarkble, however, was that it wasn't a story, but two and a half years of your young life. A living breathing human being, you stood befor us modest and eager, and recounted the horrors you had experienced, free of embellishments and exaggerations. You looked at us with the same eyes that watched those you knew and loved be ruthlessly murdred, and occasionally drummed on the podium the same fingers that pilfered bits and pieces of

Here I am telling my story as a docent at the Maltz Museum of Jewish Heritage in Beachwood, Ohio, in 2011.

bread on the fridge. I did not feel worthy of such a gift, one beyond my level of comprehension. A firsthand retelling by someone who was actually there, alive and present during one of history's most atrocious exhibits of inhumanity. By sharing your memories, however painful they may be, you have given a timeless gift to me, to us, and to the world, for you have been a part of shaping the conscience of the upcoming generation to prevent such calamities from reoccuring. I will pass your story, down to both my children and theirs, knowing that in my own, small way, I have changed the world for better. You showed me that yesterday. My admiration for you is endless.

Sincerely,

[MB]

[Hathaway Brown School, Shaker Heights, OH]

Dear Mrs. Gold,

My reaction to hearing your story was pure shock. I could not think about or even try to fathom all that you had gone through. Truthfully, I don't think that I want to fathom the emotions, the pure horror, especially, that you must have felt. If I am able to relate at all to those feelings then I will know that the world is in a very bad place as it was when you were living out the horrible tale.

I really want to thank you, Mrs. Gold, for being willing to tell us your story. All those terrible memories must be very hard to talk about. Even now, as I remember sitting there in complete shock and rapt attention to what you were saying, I cannot imagine how much braver it would take to be able to tell those stories. I do not know if it gets easier to tell the stories over time, or if it is still hard as it was the first time you had to relive the years that you spent in the woods, cold and afraid. Does time really heal the wounds? Did time heal yours? Or are they still as fresh as if it were yesterday?

That night when I was helping my mom make dinner, she asked me to go get bread from the freezer because we didn't have any in our kitchen. In the freezer we had three loaves of bread. I stood there, staring at the bread, and re-membered everything that you told us just that morning. To me that was the most powerful part of actually hearing your speech; I had realized how much I took for granted, like three loaves of bread, and how important those three loaves really were.

Sincerely,

[HB]

[Hathaway Brown School, Shaker Heights, OH]

Ms. Gold,

My name is [SK]. You spoke at the Cleveland Public Library on May 15, 2005 to a group of Chaminade Julienne [Dayton, OH] students. Your story about the Holocaust has touched my life. I remember your story, especially about you making a bet about strawberries and a quart of cream. You told the story with such grace and strength. I want to say thank you. Thank you for taking your tragic story and teaching a lesson about how precious life is. I remember sitting with about twenty or so other classmates listening to your story. The detail you gave made me feel as though I were there with you. I began to cry as my mind felt your pain. I approached you after and you kindly handed me a tissue and your card.

Over the last four years your story and strength has been in my thoughts. You have touched my life and made a positive impact. I am currently enrolled at Sinclair Community College [Dayton], studying criminal justice and sociology. I lost my older brother last year to a drunk driver. It was then that I really learned the value of life. So for that, I apologize in the delay for this thanks.

Please remember that you have made a great impact on my life as a 20 year old. Thanks.

I hope all is well with you and that you find happiness in each day. Wishing you peace and joy today and always.

With great thanks and appreciation,

[SK]

Let us never forget. I am sure I won't.

Dear Mrs. Gold,

What a phenomenal experience for me and my class. To be able to hear the story of someone who was really there [Holocaust] and survived through that most horrific and heartbreaking time in history. Once again your words and experiences have inspired and greatly affected others. It is a wonderful honor to be one of the people who heard the words of a Holocaust survivor not on tape, not on video, but almost face to face. But one thing I love the most is the fact that you did not let your past interfere with your future. You became a successful businesswoman, a loving mother, and a caring grandmother. But these are merely a few of your achievements, only the ones I know of.

After hearing you speak and telling us your story, there is no doubt in the world that your accomplishments prove Hitler and his Nazis wrong. You got your life back on track and used your tear-filled past to inspire other generations to stand up towards hate and discrimination. Thank you so much!

From one inspired,

[RS]

[Saint Joan of Arc School, Chagrin Falls, OH]

Dear Mrs. Betty Gold,

My experiences in coming to the Maltz Museum were very moving. Coming from a family of German decent, I myself was shocked and at the same time disgusted with how cruel the Nazis were to the Jewish communities across the world. . . .

I then at the time put myself in Jewish shoes. How I might feel in this situation if I was truly experiencing it. I could not come up with any words to depict these feelings. I was speechless, confused, and sick to my stomach. How could anybody on this earth do such a horrible and inhumane thing? How could these murderers live with themselves after they took innocent lives in such disgusting ways just because of their religion, what they believed, and what they preached? I find myself dumbfounded now on how much hate a human being could have.

My all time favorite part of the tour was the "Hate Room." It made me realize even to this day how much hate and discrimination there is in the world. In addition, how real terrorism truly is. . . .

I would like to close by saying that your presentation really made me realize how much terror was instilled among your people, especially with the killing of the baby to keep everyone safe. I could not even begin to imagine what I would do in these situations, nor the feelings that I would feel emotionally and physically. Keep on giving your presentation and raise more awareness of all this hate, and the struggles that you faced as a young Jewish child during this horrible era. It truly makes me think of what really happens. Also what could happen in the future if people continue to discriminate and hate. . . .

Sincerely,

[JZ]

[Valley Forge High School, Parma Heights, OH]

Dear Betty Gold,

In my entire life, I don't think that I have ever met someone who is as brave as you are. At a very young age, you had the bravery that few could very possess. You have experienced horrors that no one should ever have to experience. I wanted to thank you for sharing your experiences, and for devoting your time to the Maltz Museum. Your courage from a very young age is nothing short of inspiring and empowering.

I lost my grandfather to cancer in late April. His passing was the first instance where I had to handle the loss of someone very close to me. My grandpa meant the world to me, and his death was absolutely devastating. I still cry when I think of him being out of my life. However, I am thankful that he went peacefully. I am also thankful that I was not able to see him pass. I could not possibly imagine seeing my grandfather, who I loved more than anything, killed because he happened to be Jewish. I could not imagine seeing my parents, or my brother, who mean more than life to me, suffer. I simply could not fathom the idea of any of them suffering. If I could not handle the peaceful death of my grandpa, then I don't know how I would be able to endure what you and millions of others have gone through. Your bravery is truly inspiring to me and to anyone that would hear your experiences. I am honored that I could meet a wonderful person like you.

When Mrs. [K] told us that we were going to the Maltz Museum, I had mixed feeling. On one hand, I was scared. I had learned about the Holocaust in the past and came out of lessons afraid. When you hear about the Nazis and death camps, you cannot help but wonder "what if it were me or my family?" It scares you to think that man can be so evil. For all we know, the one who would get a Nobel Prize, who would discover a new element, who would be the next Bill Gates, was murdered by the Nazis. It's a disturbing thought that unsettles you to the point where you lie awake at night, wondering "what if?"

On the other hand, I was curious. I knew that no matter how difficult the stories were to hear, it was something that we all had to know. I knew that I would be happy that we went, and that I got to meet you, because it would positively affect my life. And it did. Although the Holocaust can make you so easily lose hope for mankind, your story has made me have hope for mankind, if that makes any sense. You hear the evils of the Nazis and you think "how can man be so evil?" How can a human being shoot another human being for no logical reason?" It makes you lose hope in humanity. THEN you look at those victims of the most evil acts in history. People like you, who are kind and brave and wonderful people that share their story with other generations. People like you give hope to humanity. . . .

Once again, I would like to thank you for the bravery you have, and for sharing your experiences. You are a wonderful human being, and it was an honor to meet you. I shall never forget your story, nor will I forget your courage. It surpasses any that I have ever seen. You are a remarkable person, and I am beyond glad that I got to meet you.

Sincerely,

[MK]

ACKNOWLEDGMENTS

The following are gratefully recognized for their assistance and inspiration: Nancy Wilhelm for encouraging Betty to have someone write her memoir and for persuading me to be that writer; Avrom Bendavid-Val, author of *The Heavens Are Empty: Discovering the Lost Town of Trochenbrod,* for his scholarship and support; Jeremy Goldscheider for producing a documentary film on Trochenbrood that featured Betty; Jonathan Safran Foer for fictionalizing Trochenbrod in *Everything Is Illuminated;* the staff at the Maltz Museum of Jewish Heritage for allowing Betty to share her story with so many visitors over the years; Saint Ignatius High School for regularly welcoming Betty to campus to speak to students; Beit Tal, United States Holocaust Memorial Museum, and USC Shoah Foundation Institute for providing background on the Holocaust; Joyce Harrison for her belief in the project.

BIBLIOGRAPHY

Beit Tal—Trochenbrod and Lozisht Coommunity (2007). http://bet-tal.com.

Bendavid-Val, Avrom. *The Heavens Are Empty: Discovering the Lost Town of Trochenbrod.* New York: Pegasus Books, 2010.

Hernandez, Nelson. "Town Lives Only in Memory." *Washington Post,* April 14, 2008.

Holocaust History Project. "Ukrainians and the Holocaust (2010)" www.holocaust-history.org.

Karfeld, Marilyn. "Film of Vanished Shtetl Reprises Woman's Story." *Cleveland Jewish News,* September 1, 2008.

Reich, Walter. "The Men Who Pulled the Triggers." *New York Times,* April 12, 1992.

COAUTHOR BIOGRAPHY

This is Mark Hodermarsky's sixth book. He has edited or authored the following titles: *The Cleveland Sports Legacy Since 1945; The Cleveland Sports Legacy, 1900–1945; The Toe: The Lou Groza Story* (with Lou Groza); *The Object of the Game* (with Charles Kyle); and *Baseball's Greatest Writers*. Hodermarsky has contributed articles to a variety of publications, including the Cleveland *Plain Dealer* and *Saint Ignatius Magazine*. He teaches English at Saint Ignatius High School in Cleveland, Ohio.

INDEX